Phoenix Park

A Novel by Gabriel Wood

Published by Excalibur Publications 2008

Copyright © Gabriel Wood 2008

Gabriel Wood has asserted his right under the Copyright, Designs and Patents Act 1988 to be identified as the author of this work

This book is sold subject to the condition that it shall not, by way of trade or otherwise, be lent, resold, hired out, or otherwise circulated without the publisher's prior consent in any form of binding or cover other than that in which it is published and without a similar condition, including this condition, being imposed on the subsequent purchaser

First published in Great Britain in 2008 by
Excalibur Publications
14 Kinlet Road
Nottingham NG5 5JT

ISBN 978-0-9559901-0-6

*For Sophie
who gave me the encouragement to
go back and sort out the things
I didn't finish in the past*

*And for Bethany
who's brought a whole new
world of possibilities to the future*

Plus ça change, plus c'est la même chose

20 November 2006
... Prologue

It all begins and ends at Phoenix Park.

Not a real park, of course, just a business park. It also serves as the terminus of the tramline from the city and houses the corporate offices of one of the major power providers in the region. By day it's home to thousands of employees, company men and women, countless hordes of telesales operatives whose job is to convince people like me that life would be a far happier place once I switch my electricity supply. But it's just a place where people work and at two-thirty in the morning all of this detail is simply irrelevant background information.

So I'm sitting on the grassy bank of some traffic island, staring intently at a huge horizontal stone altar that seems to me like it shouldn't be there at all, part of a miniature Stonehenge where the druids got bored after laying the first stone and gave up. It's been a long night filled with far too many bars, far too many beers and, after a short stop-off to re-stock, two bottles too many of Scotch. Not really my drink of choice as I don't normally have the stomach for spirits, but tonight is special, a celebration of something or other I can't properly remember, and an excuse for me to get well and truly pissed.

Out here under the stars it's cold and dark, though the alcohol keeps the former at bay and the darkness is exactly what I want right now. I could hide out here until dawn, dodging the occasional roving security guard and staring out at the city I've lived in for more than a decade. It's cold, it's dark and I'm drunk and I'll probably catch pneumonia and it's all down to a girl.

Thanks a bunch, Cassie Barclay.

Cassandra Louise Barclay. The twenty-seven year old daughter of a wealthy, self-made businessman with a job doing advertising and promotions work for daddy-dearest. The love of my life and the only thing that's kept me going for the last four years.

Cassie Barclay, who spat out a handful of words, brought my life crashing down around me and turned out to be as unreliable as everyone else in this twisted, waste-of-time world. Even now I can still hear the scorn in her voice, the mockery and laughter and worst of all, that look on her face, the way her lips changed and hardened, never wanting to be kissed by me again. I thought I knew her better than anyone else on the planet and once again fate proves that I have absolutely no idea whatsoever when it comes to figuring out women.

So it's just me and a couple of near-empty bottles of Scotch, slouching here, staring at this increasingly malevolent rock, wondering about all the times in my life when I turned left instead of right, when I said yes instead of no and how I seem to always, without fail, make the wrong decision every time I have a choice. I wonder if the druids will come back for their stone-thing, and if they do, will they decide to use me as their first sacrifice to the moon goddess or, worse still, just laugh and point and comment on how I really can't hold down a relationship to save my life.

At least I'll always have my self-pity.

"It could all have been different."

The voice in my head sounds like Cassie, but distant and washed out. I have the whole thing pinned down as just a drunken moment until I realise that someone is out here in the dark with me, in the shadows, leaning against the other side of the rock.

"What makes you so well-informed?" I ask, trying to focus on a girl's voice that never seems quite real and probably belongs to nothing more than an insubstantial genie conjured from a bottle of whisky.

"You've been talking to yourself for the past two hours. I couldn't help but overhear."

"You should have spoken up sooner. You could have shared my drink." I look at the two bottles lying on the grass by my feet. "There're a couple of mouthfuls left if you want some."

A woman steps up from her hiding place and glides round into the moonlight and suddenly things are very, very weird. It's sometime in the early hours of a cold November night and this woman, silver in the pale glow of the moon, is completely naked. What makes things worse is that every time I try to focus on her face or her body, it just blurs. I look disparagingly at the bottles and wonder why I never bothered to get this drunk before. The hallucinations are certainly worth the hangover I'm going to have in the morning. Granted, a little less smudginess and a bit more detail wouldn't go amiss, but I can't have everything and-

"You're rambling," she says, hopping up on to the giant druid-stone and stretching out on the cold rock as if it were a particularly comfy chaise longue. "I'm here to offer you a choice and if you're not careful you'll miss it."

I'm suddenly on my feet, unsteady as hell and no more than a foot away from this woman and even this close to her she's no less vague than before. "You," I manage to say even though my throat is suddenly parched, "are one very indistinct, but very naked, woman. If you're about to make me an offer then I'm unlikely to refuse, but you should know that I spent my last cash on the bottles there, and I might not be in much of a state to perform."

And I'm so drunk through all of this that the only thing I can think of is Cassie Barclay and I have no idea when this girl decided to grow an enormous pair of swan wings out of her back. My legs give out on me and the next thing I know, I'm face-down in the grass and she's crouching next to me, her perfectly formed silvery-blue feet the only things I can see.

"Julian, I want you to listen to me very carefully. You have a very important choice to make."

She knows my name and I'm so drunk that I really don't have a clue what's going on. So very, horribly drunk. "Take me home, Cassie. Please?"

"You've made mistakes, Julian, lots of horrible, stupid mistakes. I have the power to offer you the chance to put things right."

"You're giving me a second chance? Okay, get me home safely and I promise I'll never drink again. I'll do all the housework and everything. Though I should warn you that I think I'm going to be sick fairly soon."

"Listen, Julian. You can wake up tomorrow alone and with the worst hangover of your short and pitiful life, or you can take me up on my offer and actually make a difference. Which do you want?"

Short *and* pitiful? "At least I've survived longer than Jesus did." I manage to say. It's another of those 'right or left' situations. I must be just minutes away from another startlingly wrong choice.

I try to look at her again, but it's all just swimming and blurring and I'm fighting against the nausea in my stomach that's reminding me again that I don't do spirits.

And as I'm throwing up on the grass I'm murmuring things to myself. I'll do whatever it takes, just make it stop. I feel worse than I've ever felt before in my life. Take me home. Take me back. I'll make everything all right, I promise.

And as I pass out all I can think is that it all begins and ends at Phoenix Park.

Seventies

1970

As mankind finally shrugs away the sixties and pushes forward into a brave new decade, China and that electronically backward country, Japan finally manage to get themselves some satellites into orbit whilst in Europe the Anglo-French Concorde project finally gets off the ground, heralding a first-class, supersonic air service that would sadly end in flames just north of Paris some thirty years in the future.

Adding to the marvels of retro-technology, the insane Apollo space programme continues apace and the Americans send three more guys to the moon in little more than a dustbin powered by something slightly less powerful than a ZX80 home computer. Unfortunately, on the thirteenth of April something explodes and the unluckily named 'Apollo 13' mission goes horribly wrong. Thanks to the calm head of Tom Hanks in space and the tenacious sticking power of Gary Sinise at Mission Control, the crew all make it back in one piece.

Also in America, in a desperate attempt to show that it's not all space flights and roses, President Nixon was ordering troops into Cambodia on the off-chance that there might be some Vietnamese Weapons of Mass Destruction knocking about there or, as they were known back then, 'yellow, slant-eyed commies, who look a bit different to us'. And in a bold move the US Army finally lets some girlies become Generals, probably because all the regular man-troops who could have been promoted had been killed in Vietnam.

Or possibly Cambodia.

This is the world I was born into. And following hot on the heels of the break-up of The Beatles, I find myself inexplicably present at a hospital in Leicester, finally being given the chance to hear my father's immortal words as my mother is rushed into labour...

18 September 1970
... When I Find Myself in Times of Trouble

"My God, man! They killed Hendrix!"

These are the words my father is uttering as I squeeze my way into the world. At this exact moment as I fight for my first breath and become the next casualty of the miracle of life, as my mother lays sweating and screaming in the delivery room, my dad is holding a newspaper, missing it all, focussed on the untimely death of an overdosed, American guitarist. Throughout my entire life I'd never realised that Hendrix died on the exact same day I was born and though I'd never really had much interest in the guy, at this moment, standing here, I finally understand that on some basic level I always knew that my father cared more about Jimi Hendrix than he did about me. As a young child I remembered hearing my mother tell her friends the story about how she had to go to the Registry Office in secret to get my birth certificate sorted out because my dad was going to insist on calling me 'James Hendrix Grant'. Until now, I always thought she was exaggerating.

"Nobody killed Hendrix!" I yell, trying to pull the paper from him and direct his gaze to the more urgent events taking place. "I'm sure if you look into it properly you'll find he just took too many drugs or something. The guy simply didn't know when to stop having a good time!"

"No, my friend, that's exactly what they want you to believe!

They're getting rid of the free-thinkers! They're killing-off humanity's poets! I just can't get over this, man! First they kill the Beatles, now they take out Jimi! It's the end of the world, man! End of the fucking world!"

This is without a doubt the most important day of my life, my actual, honest-to-goodness, 'birthday'. And my dad's missing it all.

I need to try and focus him. Grabbing him on either side of his head I stare into his dilated eyes and quietly, clearly, let him have the facts. "Dave. 'Man'. Firstly, no one killed the Beatles, they just split up and went their separate ways. Secondly, your beloved Jimi was constantly off his face and it was only a matter of time before he went too far and killed himself and thirdly, and some might say most importantly, you've just missed the birth of your firstborn son. Now get in there and give Jenny some attention!"

Something finally clicks in his head and he starts to nod. "You're right, man. I'll do that now. Go and see the new little kid, huh? There'll be plenty of time later to get to work on exposing the government's involvement in the Hendrix death case."

I shake my head. Right now, it isn't worth the worry.

When I originally arrived back in 1970 my first idea was to track down my parents and somehow become a friend of the family so I could keep an eye on myself whilst I was growing up. It took me no time at all to find the fairly quiet suburb of Leicester and the house where I grew up with my parents, David Grant and Jennifer Saxton. I never really saw that many photos of my family from the early days and even though I always knew that I was born when they were hardly past twenty years old, the shock of finding myself more than a decade older than my parents was still fairly considerable.

I arranged things so I could accidentally bump into them at a local pub, The Mangled Pheasant, (possibly not it's true name), where I got chatting about the horrendous price of beer these days and they nodded sagely and introduced themselves. I told them I was from Nottingham, down in Leicester for a few months to look for work and get a change of scenery following an unhappy relationship breakup. It wasn't until after I told them this to them that I finally realised it was all too true and that yes, I had just got out of a major relationship. More importantly, since Cassie Barclay, the bane of my life, wouldn't be born for nearly ten years, I really did need to focus on finding some work soon or my landlady was going to start getting a seriously miffed.

There wasn't a lot I could do about it at nine at night in the lounge bar of a grimy pub though, so I got some more drinks in and got myself a little better acquainted with the people my parents used to be before I turned up and changed their lives forever.

Jennifer was, despite being heavily pregnant, a fairly slim blonde, somewhat quiet and detached, who spent her free time painting abstract pictures which in her words were 'an indictment of the current world order and a celebration of the power of the masses'. Seeing her here and now, young and pretty and with her whole life stretching out before her, made it difficult for me to reconcile this person with what I knew of her the future. Every so often I would catch myself just staring at the bump in her belly and she'd smile, all happy and proud to be giving someone their best possible start in life. I may well have been getting a bit drunk, but finding myself in two places at the same time was a quite bizarre experience.

Dave was the exact opposite of Jenny. The father I knew had always been a sombre, brooding man who never seemed too worried about, well... anything really, but seeing him here as a long-haired kid was as shocking to me as waking up one morning and finding myself suddenly female. I know people change as they get older and settle down. Virtually everyone gets quieter and calmer. When I was his age I was certainly more of a rebel than I am now, but when I actually met him face to face, I was nothing short of stunned. My dad, the sober, patient, well-considered adult, was a twenty-two year old guy who thought he was Dennis Hopper from Easy Rider. It takes a bit of getting used to. Especially the half-baked American accent he was always putting on and even more especially, the cowboy hat that never left his head.

I got along well with both of them from the start and although I only arrived here a month ago, we've become good friends. I keep my mouth shut about the future, partly because I don't want to be locked up for being a loony, but mainly because I never really know what to say anyway. I get a feeling in my stomach that it would be better all round if we just play things out and see where life leads us.

Today, on the day of my birth, I'm considered a good enough friend to hold my dad's hand at the hospital. To be honest, the rest of the people he knew didn't seem all that reliable and his only brother was travelling in Europe somewhere and no one really knew where to find him, (although from what I heard at various family gatherings, good old Uncle Bernie was probably making his way to the commune in Italy where he did enough experimental drugs and wild sex to ensure that his exploits were still being talked about by morally-offended relatives even in my day).

So it's down to me to make sure that Dave doesn't pass out at the birth or offer the newborn something to smoke or generally, as Jenny so neatly put it, 'fuck things up'.

I push him though the doors and into the delivery room, stopping momentarily to grab the newspaper from him and follow him over to where my mother lays, recuperating.

"Hey, how are you feeling?" I ask, before Dave can start up about Hendrix once again. "We caught it all from the window, I'm afraid Dave's stomach wasn't up to being any closer."

Still recovering, a weak smile is all she manages and it's so difficult to keep back from this tiny version of myself and let Dave have his moment. He's finally staring at the little baby cradled in its mother's arms and there's a look on his face that I can only assume passes for pride under the bushy and overgrown Hopper-esque moustache. This is their day, anticipated, planned for, longed for and dreaded for the best part of nine months. Their lives are turned upside-down and everything they do from now on will be coloured by the fact that they are responsible for the happiness and safety of another human being.

For a moment or two I futilely try to combine the words 'responsibility' and 'Dave' in the same sentence, but eventually give up. At least Jenny appears to have her head screwed on and now they have me around to help out too.

Dave has his finger grasped in the little me's hand and is smiling and, for just this moment, he doesn't have a care in the world. Everything is fine. Even Hendrix is shoved to the back of his mind. I can't help looking at me and feeling that three and a half decades of my history have been wiped out. Anything is possible again. Things could be so different this time.

Jenny looks up at me from the bed, smiling through the exhaustion of a ten hour labour marathon. "We were stuck for a name. I was always going to call my first child Mary, after my mother, but that doesn't seem too appropriate now. And I don't think you want to know what Dave wants to call him! We could never really manage to agree on a boy's name but we did start to wonder, after that first time we met you and, well, would you mind if we named him after you?"

It shouldn't be a surprise really, but I'm so touched I have to wipe at my eyes before I kneel down next to the bed and hesitantly run a finger along the side of his tiny sleeping head. "Hey, little Julian," I whisper. "Welcome to the world."

"We were also wondering if you'd be his godfather?" Jenny is serious as she says this, offering the protection of their only child to someone they've only just met, but who they somehow implicitly trust. "Nothing deep and religious, just someone to take care of him should anything happen to us."

I look at them both, happy and proud parents with the foresight to plan for the unexpected. They've invited me into their lives, trusted me with their son, and given me the chance to start putting a few things straight.

"Hey," I say, my voice dropping low and husky, my best attempt at a New York-Italian accent. "You're making me an offer I cannot refuse."

Their blank looks make me wonder just how bad my impressions have become and then it hits me again where I am and that Coppola's masterpiece won't be released for another two years.

"Don't worry," I smile. "I'll look after him as though his life were my own."

1970 – 1971

As the world continues to wonder just what, exactly, the whole Vietnam War is actually about, President Nixon bolsters support by hitting the road and performing his 'Lock Up Your Daughters' European tour. The tour comprises of a combination of stand-up routines, musical numbers and mime and was a smash hit throughout Italy, Yugoslavia, Spain, Ireland and particularly the United Kingdom, where his V-sign fingers reminded everyone of the hero of the Second World War, Winston Churchill.

Unwilling to be upstaged, Pope Paul VI follows this up with his 'Give Peace a Chance' gig, which toured Asia and Australia and featured a cutting-edge laser-light show and some very clever anti-war satire written by His Holiness himself. Sadly, Pope Paul has nothing to match the vote winning power of Nixon's V-fingers and his tour is forced to close down early.

Back home in Britain, war was the furthest thing from anyone's mind as Decimalisation Day hits and everyone is given brand-spanking new coins to play with. The new one-hundred-pence-to-the-pound system was tricky for the elderly to adopt as they were much happier with their old money in which there were twelve pence in a shilling and twenty shillings to the pound, and hence two hundred and forty pence in a pound, which is clearly much better value. Only recently deprived of such unintelligible coins as the guinea, the thrupenny bit, the farthing, the crown and the half-crown, the elderly revolted but found the government unsympathetic to their pain.

When asked for a statement, an anonymous Bank of England clerk said, "We just don't care. The pensioners of today are a dying breed."

3 July 1971
... Riders on the Storm

The campaign headquarters of the Jimi Hendrix Revival Movement was based in the bedroom of Steve Johnson who, at the age of twenty-six, was still living with his parents, Irene and Graham in a small terrace house in a suburb of Leicester not far from Dave and Jenny's place.

Steve was one of Dave's more reliable mates who would always arrange to be places and never turn up, would agree to help out on things then remember he had other plans and generally never be where he said he'd be at any point in time. He was a strange choice for hosting the Hendrix Revival, but insisted that this was exactly what he wanted and that he needed to play a bigger role in things these days.

Since last September the ad-hoc meetings had been held here and staggeringly Steve had ensured that he was always around when he was needed. His life now had a purpose and that purpose was guiding the Revival and promoting new ways of proving that Hendrix was assassinated by government agents who didn't want 'filthy, long-haired, hippie scum' contaminating the streets of England.

Although Steve was the host of the meetings, my dad was always the leader, guiding, co-ordinating and adding the required amounts of passionate rhetoric to any potentially volatile situation. He also felt it was really, really important to have a good catch phrase. "Moral oppression, man," was one of Dave's favourites at Revivalist meetings. I'm not sure it actually meant anything to him, or to anyone else for that matter, but he said it often enough to be convincing and it gave him another chance to end yet another sentence with the word 'man'.

It was strange to think that my dad would change so much over the coming years. As far back as the early eighties I remember him being a quiet, well behaved guy. He was the sort of person that geese said 'boo' to. Things had changed by then, of course. He was alone, my mother was no longer around and he had me and my sister to look after. I suppose, deep down, everyone knows when it's time to hang up your masks, disguises and Dennis Hopper hats and become who you need to be to survive, especially when there are people relying on you to keep them from going hungry. Here in the seventies I'm looking at a different, more alive Dave Grant and keep finding myself battling with an overwhelming urge to steal his hat and hide it somewhere. It's childish, I know, but I've never claimed to make excuses for my behaviour.

Meanwhile, back here in the bedroom at number fifteen Lombard Crescent, the usual crew of Revivalists are assembling. Dave is here with Jenny, who really has no idea why they pursue this ridiculous course of action, but stands by her man as his loyal and loving wife. Little Julian is here with them and, though he sleeps for most of the time, he occasionally wakes up and cries until he gets fed, which Jenny does by casually popping one of her breasts out in front of everyone and letting the other me suckle away merrily. I may not be all that clued-up on motherhood, but I'm almost a year old now and I'm not sure I still need to be breast-fed in public and no matter how weird you think it might be for me to see myself sucking one of my mother's nipples, the reality is a dozen time more disturbing.

But I'm digressing from the militant action at hand.

Beside Dave is Steve, who has been holding these meetings almost every other Saturday evening between seven and nine whilst his parents are out at Bingo. One week back in February the Bingo was cancelled at short notice and to hide the fact that he was hosting an anti-establishment meeting of pop-culture rebels, Steve insisted we all spend the evening downstairs with his parents, watching Morecambe and Wise, drinking sherry and discussing the possibility of power-cuts and union strike action. To be honest there was an unusual element of 'family' there that I hadn't seen in a long time, but even so, spending time watching an old black and white Eric and Ernie show with someone's parents is not my idea of a good time and it didn't help us nail the government dictators who killed Hendrix either.

During that two-hour long visit to purgatory, I counted Dave say 'moral oppression, man' fifteen times, every utterance of which causing an involuntary spasm in Mrs Johnson's neck muscles.

Back in Steve's bedroom, hunched up in the corner on the bed are Diane and Pete. I try not to have too much to do with them since as far as I can tell they're nothing more than very bad accidents waiting to happen. I get the impression that they're the sort of couple who'd love to become actual terrorists or mercenaries or something, but only so they could actually get to blow things up and not because they have any beliefs to promote or points to make. Pete has been in prison at sometime or other for attempted armed robbery and so far as I can tell, Diane makes a living through a mixture of dole fraud and providing sexual favours for Pete's 'business contacts'. And though I can't be certain, I think they've taken some sort of medical-grade amphetamine because neither of them have blinked in over ten minutes and Dave is staring at me like I'm his next meal.

Other than me the final member of our little cell is Viv, a rabid, shaven headed, extreme left-wing, pro-life, anti-war, Buddhist-anarchist lesbian with a badly hidden secret ambition to kill everyone in the government in a jihad of bloody vengeance. I may be exaggerating a little here, but the one thing I've learned from my short time in the past is that the seventies really is populated entirely by stereotypes.

And finally there's me. I've given up trying to convince Dave that there's no government conspiracy and that there were, in fact, a lot of drug-taking rock stars queuing up at this time to meet their maker. I've decided to throw in my lot and back them a whole hundred percent. We can fight the system and show the fascists the error of their ways and all the time I can spend quality hours with my younger-than-me parents before they turn into, well, someone's parents.

Right on, man. Power to the people.

There's an electric air in the room tonight and everyone knows that this meeting is bigger than most. Steve takes the chair and, as he does every other week welcomes us to the meeting. Dave has today's newspaper in his lap and although I know he wants to make an impact, everyone already knows what this meeting is going to be about.

Steve looks around at everyone and ticks off their names on a clipboard pad that he brings out every week for taking minutes. I have to admit that for a rebelling anarchist wanting to overthrow the government and return the reins of power to the workers he's incredibly well structured and business-like. It's such a shame he has another fifteen years to wait until he can embrace the regimented, corporate values of the mid-eighties.

"Okay, people. Welcome to today's meeting of the Hendrix Revival. Obviously we have a lot to discuss today so how about we give the meeting over to Dave, who I know has a few points to put forward. Dave?"

In an unparalleled gesture, Dave stands up, actually removes his hat, and unfurls the newspaper for all to see.

"This, man," he says, pointing at the grainy black and white photo splashed on the cover of The Mirror, "is extreme moral oppression."

That's the first one, I count whilst taking in the photo of Jim Morrison, found this morning in his bath, dead at the age of twenty-seven. Like everyone else in the room I'd read about it earlier and seen it on the news. Morrison moved to Paris to begin a new clean-living lifestyle only to suffer a heart attack in the bath that was in no way drink or drug related.

"We have a growing situation," he continues, "where Parliament refuses to admit that these atrocities are being carried out at their own behest. And worse still, the French government are now clearly managing their own execution programme, possibly co-ordinated with the British plan. We have to strike now, before someone else is targeted. If we aren't careful we're going to have more deaths over the coming months and, as the only people in this country who seem capable of seeing the truth, I think we need to take a more active stand against this oppression. I ask the group for possible strategies of attack."

Dave drops down in his seat and drops his hat back on his head.

Steve scribbles something on his clipboard and addresses the rest of us.

"So, how many agree with Dave?"

One by one, all the hands are raised and Dave even lifts little Julian's arm up to add to the unanimous vote. It seems that, one way or another, I'm with them too. I figure that at worst we write some letters to MPs and at best we perhaps set up a protest march to London to gain media coverage. Stupid as either option seems, there's loads more fun to be had here than there is sitting at home and staring at a television set that only has three channels.

"So," Steve carries on, "last month we wrote to the Prime Minister's office again demanding an investigation into the split of The Beatles and the death of Hendrix. This was our twentieth such letter and to date none have been dignified with a reply. We also petitioned them to rename September the eighteenth as 'Hendrix Day', which is apparently sitting in their 'pending consideration' pile. I could be wrong, but I'm not sure we're being taken seriously. Any suggestions?"

Dave is shaking his head, muttering "moral oppression, man" under his breath. Little Julian is starting to cry and it disturbingly looks as if Jenny is about to try and feed him again.

Viv raises her hand and offers her latest piece of clever advice.

"After we heard about them getting to Morrison this morning, Diane and me got talking and have decided it's time to get back at them. We had a few ideas, ran them by Pete and, assuming you wouldn't mind, we've put a few things in place."

Steve is feverishly taking notes, a look of intense glee on his face.

Dave scratches at his moustache, clearly interested. "What kind of things?"

Suddenly the room is Plot Headquarters. I can hear the theme to mission impossible start up in my head and it's like the bit from a heist movie where the plan is being laid out with accompanying graphics, lots of close-ups and zooms, CGI schematics of the casino to be hit and plenty of frenzied cutting between the various body parts of each of the protagonists.

"We get them back for Hendrix, Morrison and The Beatles in one shot," she says. "For every one of ours they've killed, we'll take out one of theirs. We've been looking at things and there's not much going on for the next few days, so we've decided that we can all take a couple of days off work, head down to London and take down our targets, yeah?"

The camera pans round to me, holding my finger in the air as I raise what I consider to be a reasonably pertinent question. "You do realise, Viv, that The Beatles aren't actually dead?"

Zoom back to Viv, fast close up on her eyes as she slowly shakes her head.

"Oh, you couldn't be more wrong, Julian." And as if that explains everything, she moves on. "Diane has the next part of the plan."

There's an overhead shot of Diane, pulling a folded piece of paper from her blouse and spreading it out on the floor. "This is a map of the centre of London with the main objectives marked on it in felt-tip." She starts stabbing her finger at three red crosses that are large enough to obscure any map details that may be useful to the plan.

"Here, 10 Downing Street." Stab. "This, Parliament." Stab. "And this-" Stab. "Harrods. Pete?"

A sweeping camera change to Pete, slouched on the bed, propped against the wall, his dirty red T-shirt emblazoned with a badly rendered image of Hendrix's face. He seems miles away from the room and in a monotone regurgitates his part of the plan like he's reading from cue cards.

"We head to London tomorrow and plant bombs at each of these locations on Monday the Prime Minister will pass the end of Downing Street by car and we blow him to bits on Tuesday the Foreign Secretary is going to Parliament and we catch him and explode the second bomb as he enters the building and on Wednesday the Chancellor of the Exchequer is opening a new 'wigs and beards' section at Harrods which is a prime opportunity for us to explode bomb number three."

The camera zooms out. The room is silent.

After two stunned minutes I have to say something.

"You're suggesting we turn ourselves into actual, armed terrorists?"

"We have to make a stand." And for effect, Diane stabs her finger at the three crosses on the map once again, the last stab forcing her fingernail through the paper and into the carpet.

"You actually want to blow people up? You have bombs?"

Viv shrugs. "We get to the bastards before they can get any more of us. Pete knows people in London who can get us the bombs and by this time next week we'll be famous and targets like Dylan and the Stones will be safe! "

"But you'll get caught after the first blast, if not before! You aren't terrorists, you're a bunch of amateurs! Steve works in shoe department of Debenhams for Christ's sake! And you haven't even got any bombs and don't have a clue what you're doing! Are you planning to bring London to its knees with Diane's City and Guilds Certificate in Hairdressing? And just what have you set in place already? Nothing!"

Viv calmly pulls out her tobacco tin, starts making a roll-up and, whilst everyone ponders my outburst and begins to think that just maybe this whole plan is getting a little strange, she pulls a brown envelope from inside her jacket.

"I have six tickets to London, tomorrow morning at eight. Now who's coming with me?"

1971 – 1972

Imagine what the world would be like if it was missing two billion people. Imagine that and you have the early seventies. You can't help but look out of your window and feel that the world is a little empty. It's certainly missing a fair amount of traffic.

And all these people sitting around have no idea what's coming. Their idea of hi-tech is a phone with a dial on the front where it takes longer to dial 999 than it does to die from a heart attack or a house fire. But things are about to change.

Right now, as Britain launches its first satellite, Nixon is announcing the start of some reusable, science-fiction style space shuttle. Soon enough there will be so much monitoring and communications equipment in orbit that people will be amazed they can still see the stars.

The development of the first microchip is leading the way to affordable computers in every home. Try telling someone in 1972 that someday soon their washing machine will have more processing power than the onboard computer of an Apollo spacecraft. I tried it. People laughed. I didn't dare start explaining the internet.

In America, the world's first pocket calculator is unveiled. It costs approximately one month's salary and has a whopping thirty-five buttons. Even so, the most important, most used function will still be to enter the number five million, three hundred and eighteen thousand and eight and turn the calculator upside-down.

And in New York a guy is making the first mobile phone call, signalling the start of an age where people can stay in touch no matter where they are, day or night.

And this is just the beginning...

17 September 1972
... A Long, Long Time Ago,
I Can Still Remember

As expected, the trip down to London was a real blast and everything was over by Monday teatime and, as I lay here in bed over a year later, events drift back to me again like a recurring nightmare from which there's no escape.

Dave, Jenny, Myself, Pete, Diane and Viv were the attack team while Steve stayed at home since he had to spend Sunday lunch with his parents, which at least meant that someone could look after my younger self whilst we were away attempting acts of public terrorism.

I met Dave and Jenny at their house and we made our way to the station to meet the others at seven thirty. Dave had packed a Thermos of coffee and a selection of sandwiches for the journey down. There were four cheese and onion, four beef paste and four with luncheon meat and mustard to ensure that everyone's tastes were fully catered for. He also had an eight-pack of Penguins in case we needed extra energy. At the station, Viv was already on the platform waiting for us and we were finally joined by Pete and Diane ten minutes before the train was due to leave.

The journey to the Capital was nothing short of boring, with Pete asleep for most of it whilst Viv and Diane disappeared off somewhere together and were barely seen. My parents were reading, Jenny making her way through a novel entitled *Under the Rainbow* and Dave alternating between a magazine called *Bike!*

and an unauthorised, posthumous biography of Jimi Hendrix going by the title *Falling Star*. I occupied myself with more historical tabloid journalism courtesy of a three-day old copy of The Sun, keeping me up to date with such significant topics as the Vietnam War and the economic impact of potential strike action on the nation. Of course these articles were merely fillers and the stories on the front page were chiefly to do with why beer should cost less, why all striking coal miners were homosexual and of course the Pulitzer Prize winning headline 'Topless Totty - See Page Three'.

Incidentally, for those who care, the topless totty in question was Carol, aged twenty from Lowestoft. Carol's interests are, incredibly, swimming, higher mathematics and global politics. 'I just want to make the world a better place and do what I can to promote peace in the Far East.' Says the bouncy secretary from England's most easterly town. Carol is five feet four inches tall, blonde and has tits the size of watermelons.

It's somewhat comforting to know that tabloid journalism is just as deep and insightful in the seventies as it will be in my day.

After three hours and one lengthy delay to remove a cow from the tracks we finally get to London where it transpires that during their extended trip to the toilet, Viv has shaved Diane's head and they now look like a matching pair of escaped convicts. Pete doesn't seem to care, or indeed notice, and heads off to a phone to make contact with his explosives supplier whilst Dave and Jenny check in with Steve to make sure little Julian isn't having any trouble without them.

And this was sort of when things got a tiny bit out of hand.

Although the baby version of me is fine and Steve is happily helping out with Sunday dinner at home, it turns out that Pete's contact has buggered off to Leeds or somewhere and won't be around until at least Thursday. The best they can do is give Pete the name of a pub in Camden where there's apparently a good chance of meeting someone called Mickey Fitch who can give him the stuff he needs. All we get out of Pete for the next hour is the repeated use of the word 'fuck', occasionally followed up with a random 'Paddy terrorist cunt' for good measure. I couldn't be entirely certain but I'm fairly sure Pete was again under the influence of some fairly major prescription-only drugs and my main concern was making sure that he didn't get too close to either myself, Dave or Jenny.

At the Highland Donkey in Camden, we all decided to stay outside and send Pete in alone to check out the place and find out if this Mickey Fitch character was around, or even to see if he actually really existed. Pete was only gone for about ten minutes and when he re-emerged he was carrying a piece of paper and swearing even worse than before. Apparently Mickey was in the business of supplying explosives and arms to various terrorist factions on both sides of the Irish border. Business was booming and we'd just missed out since he'd given out his last batch of 'the good stuff' yesterday. He did, however provide Pete with less than detailed instructions on how to mix home-made explosives and to cut the story down to the important part, we needed a load of questionable ingredients from chemists and it was a Sunday in the seventies and everywhere was closed. So we booked into a bed and breakfast and sent Diane and Viv out to see what they could come up with from any shops they could find open.

By seven o'clock they finally made it back to our rooms but sadly it seemed that they'd just spent the afternoon at Camden Market picking out some new clothes for Diane. The two of them were now almost indistinguishable and both looked like they'd spent the last year or so living rough, which was presumably the effect they were aiming for.

When Pete asked how they'd got on with the explosives shopping list, they just shrugged and handed him a carrier bag filled with eggs and flour. "Best we could do." Viv said, before again leaving the room with Diane, throwing a quick "going out, back later," over her shoulder.

There was an uneasy atmosphere left in the room and as Pete locked himself in the toilet, Dave and Jenny decided to go out for a walk and some dinner and I decided to turn in early. I stretched out on the sofa and caught what sleep I could between fevered dreams where I was being pursued through the streets of London by two naked, shaven-headed, vampire lesbians, all the time trying to figure out why I was wearing Dave's cowboy hat.

All in all, by morning I was less confident in our little team than I could have been and when we set out for the Prime Minister's house we were each armed with four flour bombs and half a dozen eggs with which to pelt his car as he passed by. "We still need to make a stand, man," was Dave's carefully planned philosophy at this time. "We have to stop them from killing anyone else!"

Needless to say, it was a shambles.

We waited for hours. There was no car carrying Mr Heath, and nothing at all that might indicate that the Prime Minister was even at home. By Lunchtime we were attracting the attention of the police stationed outside the street so we headed off for some food, went back an hour later, hurled the flour and eggs at the first car we saw, which belonged to some junior Minister for Agriculture and were chased out of Downing Street by the boys in blue.

When we finally regrouped at the bed and breakfast Dave and Pete were missing. We waited around, kept an eye on the road from the window, and by six o'clock got our answers on the news.

It seems that Dave was caught on film by a news crew hurling the flour and eggs and yelling, "Stop the moral oppression, man! Stop killing our people!" The rest of his protest went unheard as he disappeared under a mass of flailing blue-uniformed bodies. A mob of police arrived by van and Pete was grabbed, pulled a knife and made a bit of a mess of some guy's face before he was disarmed and truncheoned to the ground.

There was nothing we could do but sit and wait and when no one came looking for us the next morning we assumed we were safe. Knowing we couldn't stay in London forever, I told Jenny I'd go to the police with her to try and sort out the Dave situation and Diane told us that she was heading back to Leicester with Viv to get her things before they started out on a new life together in a commune near Market Harborough.

It took some time to find out where Dave was being held and when we finally managed to get to the police station we weren't even allowed anywhere near him and almost succeeded in getting ourselves arrested for being his accomplices. In a final disappointment the news had broadcast Dave's attack as either a protest against American involvement in Vietnam, some hippie vendetta against the establishment or, in the case of a headline in The Sun, 'Junior Minister Flour-Bombed by Secret Illegitimate Son'.

Dave got two years for causing an affray. A bit harsh, but with the IRA stepping up its activities he was being made an example of. Pete was on track for getting five years until someone pointed out his past record of criminal behaviour and it was upped to ten. At his trial it also came to light that at the time he was arrested he was completely out of his face on highly addictive, experimental horse tranquilisers.

1972 – 1973

Late in 1972 the world was hit by the first screening of the hit show *Rainbow*, a searing indictment of social politics and sexuality that would become a mainstay of kids' viewing for the next twenty years. Set in a house somewhere in England, poor, downtrodden Geoffrey suddenly finds himself living with a seven foot tall brown bear, a pink pigmy hippo and what could only be a crassly-behaved, orange alien with a zip-up mouth.

Constantly worried for his safety and fearing attack by the bear, Geoffrey made sure his house was always protected by a bunch of elite, combat-trained folk singers. The most popular of these, Rod, Jane and Freddy, kept up security for many years, but were eventually so unnerved by the bear, (who would wander around naked all day, but wear pyjamas for bed and trunks when swimming), that they left the house in 1989 and are now involved in hush-hush military ops in the Middle East.

Defence of the house was now left to a mixture of less able singers, notably the amusingly named, Christopher Lillycrap. Sadly, the bear was now unstoppable and was actively taking advantage of Lillycrap's lacklustre attitude toward safety. In 1992 the bear broke free from its cage and, wearing nothing but a bowler hat, rampaged through the streets tearing up shoppers and children until it was humanely shot in the head.

In the aftermath of all this, Geoffrey left the house and became romantically involved with his next-door neighbour Dawn and the pink hippo, George, went to live in Liverpool, once again claiming that he was not in any way interested in boys. Orange-headed Zippy was finally hunted down and captured in Wrexham, where he was taken away for scientific experimentation.

At least that's the way I remember it...

17 November 1973
... Clowns to the Left of Me, Jokers to the Right

When it became apparent that Jenny had fallen pregnant again she went to great lengths to convince me that the child wasn't mine. I went along with things, but since we'd been sleeping together on and off for the last year and a half there was a more than even chance that the child could be my kid. Of course I had worries that the genetics could be screwed up, that the child could be deformed or have six fingers on each hand, and though she did her best to convince me otherwise, I could tell Jenny was never quite one hundred percent certain that Dave was the father.

I didn't know whether to be concerned or not. Since arriving back in 1970 I'd discovered that I seemed to have the ability to change only the smallest of things and I knew from my own past that my sister, Marie, was a perfectly healthy baby who would grow up to be solicitor working in Swansea with a husband, a mortgage and two kids of her own. But there was always a nagging doubt at the back of my mind that I'd help create some kind of monster.

And today's the day that my sister is born, three and a bit years since I last stood here with Dave to witness my own birth.

Both of us are here again and this time Dave is right up there beside his wife, holding her hand and talking her through the labour. And me? I'm standing a little way back, off to one side, quietly simmering with jealousy. I seem to view the whole scene from somewhere up above my head and once more I'm alarmed at how I'm the odd one out in this scenario. I'm really not supposed to be here. Somewhere along the way I've taken a wrong turn and if I'm honest, there isn't a night goes by that I don't fall asleep thinking about how totally fucked up my life has become.

When Dave went to prison no one expected him to go through it alone and when he refused to see anyone who came to visit we thought it was just a phase he'd grow out of once he acclimatised to life behind bars. I know Jenny took it badly and everyone was worried about Dave on some level. We all desperately wanted to make his time inside pass easier. But he wouldn't let us do anything except worry about him and wait for him to come back into our lives, brimming with moral oppression, his hair a little longer his moustache a little bushier, ready to write petitions to the government and start protests outside super markets.

It was three months into Dave's sentence that Jenny started to go off the rails. She started drinking heavily, was on the verge of losing her job and had more than one caution about her behaviour from the police. I couldn't just stand by and let her destroy herself, so I stepped in, got Steve to look after Julian and took her away for a quiet week in the Peak District. I don't know if I was completely naive or secretly manipulating events without even realising. I'm fairly sure at the time I thought it was all above board when I booked separate rooms for us in a Bed and Breakfast near Matlock where we spent a lot of time just walking in the hills and chatting about how things had got out of control lately. We talked about her childhood and her parents and I made up some stories about how exciting it was to be a kid during the Second World War how Elvis had really let himself go since the fifties. She talked some more and I remained the model of an attentive and devoted listener. Any sane person with an ounce of sense would have seen what was happening from a mile away.

And I just rolled along with it like a complete idiot.

Four days into the holiday we finished dinner and were upstairs in her room, talking again about that ridiculous trip to London and how things could have turned out so differently if only we hadn't listened to everyone else's mad ideas. One minute we were laughing over the spectacle of Dave pelting random cars with flour and eggs and the next she was sobbing. She just broke down in front of me, finally crushed under the pain of bringing up a child alone and being separated from a husband who refused to even see her.

This was the woman who left me and my father before I was even ten years old, the mother I never really got a chance to know. For years I unconsciously blamed her for so much that had gone wrong in my life. At the back of my mind I always thought things would have been so much better if she'd stuck around longer. And yet here she was, so young and scared and defenceless, her family and her very existence falling apart around her and there was nothing she could do to stop it.

I should have walked away right then, as she moved in and hugged me, but I didn't. I crossed a line I hadn't even seen myself approaching. And no matter how wrong my actions may have been, I couldn't just abandon her when she needed me the most. I couldn't just leave her to fend for herself the way she had done to me such a long time ago.

So I stayed with her, and held on to her as tightly as I could.

The Dave that finally walked back into our lives last Christmas was a complete stranger. The moustache had disappeared, the hat was gone. He'd even got a haircut and a new suit. We later found out that he'd been offered a release three months earlier but had punched a fellow inmate in the face for no reason and got his sentence extended. It was like he didn't want to come home. And when he turned up in the pub that day, refusing even to be picked up from the prison, he seemed happy enough to be free, but the Dave Grant spark of passion that used to burn inside him was missing.

"You have to grow up sometime," he said to me. "My stupidity let my family down and I'm not going to go there again."

And in the back of my mind all I was wondering was, *does he know?* If he did, he kept it to himself and got on with his life. He found a job working for a large engineering firm and focussed all his energy on making a stable home for Jenny and little Julian.

And there he is now, helping his wife through her second birth, so completely different from the man I met three years ago. And I, at this moment, watching her gripping his hand, going through the birth together, I know that for Dave's sake I have to stop seeing Jenny. The man doesn't deserve to be cheated on like that.

I look over at the clock on the wall and, at 7.12pm on 17 November 1973, my sister Marie makes her way into the world. The doctors whisk her away to tidy her up and begin to murmur in hushed tones as a knot the size of a football starts to tighten in my stomach. I can see that Dave is worried. Jenny is starting to panic and is asking for her baby.

The nurse is talking urgently to Dave, making calming gestures with her hands, but I can't tell what she's saying. It's like the sound has been turned off.

I'm staring at the proceedings, panicking at the thought of my poor little sister having some problem because of me, being born a mutant because of me, and it suddenly occurs to me that I've stopped breathing and tiny lights start bursting in front of my eyes and

Dave's smiling down at me as I take in the fact that I'm in a hospital bed and my head is pounding.

"What happened?" I ask him. "I feel like I've got the world's worst hangover."

"You passed out. When you fell over you managed to smash your head against a table. They had to stitch you up and want to keep you in overnight to keep an eye on you. You know, just in case your brain fell out of the hole."

"Oh." It's still a bit hazy and I actually start to wonder if some of my brain did fall out. "How are Jenny and Marie?"

"Marie?"

There's a sinking in my stomach. Things are suddenly going horribly wrong. "The baby?"

Dave seems puzzled, but shrugs it off. "They're both fine. There was some trouble with her breathing, but it's sorted. She's fit and healthy. We haven't decided on a name yet, though. We were trying to make a decision between Catherine and Mary, after either mine or Jenny's mother."

"I must have misheard you talking while I was out."

I can tell Dave doesn't quite take my feeble remark as gospel, but since there doesn't appear to be a better explanation he lets it go.

"Marie's a good name though. I'll run it past Jenny. 'Marie Catherine'." He turns to leave. "I'll come back and check on you later. Get some rest and try not to hit your head on anything sharp."

In my half-drugged, half-dazed state it takes about five minutes for me to fall asleep again, lulled back into oblivion by the throbbing pulse in my head and before I know it I'm dreaming about the future. It's the year 2000 and everything is made of silver and people drive flying cars and have personal robots to do the housework.

I think the seventies are really starting to get to me.

The clock opposite my bed says it's half-past three and, judging by the quiet and darkness, this is the half-past three that most people don't see very often. I'm still dreaming of a future where I fly a rocket ship and everyone takes holidays in space and I imagine that Jenny is standing beside me holding Marie and watching over me in silence.

"Hi," I say, mot really knowing where things stand.

She just smiles and I get flashes of memory and images from the few photos of her taken in the years before she left my dad. I see frozen pictures of her wedding day, of a holiday by the beach with me on her knee, of a family photo from the zoo where we went for Marie's fifth birthday. Images of events that haven't even happened yet. I never really knew my mother and before this last couple of years all I had were these distant memories of someone who left us when I was so very young. And now she means more to me than anything else in the world. I try to douse my feelings for her by thinking about Cassie, but it doesn't really work. Cassie Barclay hasn't even been born yet.

"Dave and me are getting married." She says. "I just thought you should know."

I close my eyes and wait for her to leave but she just stands there and watches over me until I fall asleep again.

1973 – 1974

With the western world still recovering from the Vietnam conflict and the premature end of Richard Nixon's second term in office, the American public was left wondering just what the hell was going on with their government and praying feverishly that new President, Gerry Ford would have all the answers they were looking for. Could this be the start of a new time of stability for America? Could good, honest, US citizens sleep safer at night knowing that the days of uncertainty were finally over?

Fortunately, all of America's worries disappeared overnight when the ABC network released the hit sitcom, Happy Days, and for ten years and two hundred and fifty-five episodes everyone thought it was the 1950s again. Kennedy had never been assassinated, nobody was confused by the Nixon administration and Vietnam had never happened. Granted, there was a worrying suspicion that the Korean War was starting up again, but that was okay since the crew from *M*A*S*H* were already taking care of things over there.

And so everyone was happy, except for Richie Cunningham's older brother, Chuck, who was thinking of going off to college and was never heard from again. To this day Howard and Marion adamantly maintain that they have just the two children and never allow anyone access to their cellar.

In other news, progress is made as those wacky Americans finally remove homosexuality from their Dictionary of Mental Disorders and Swedish pop sensation ABBA wins the Eurovision Song Contest with the popular wedding-disco favourite, Waterloo...

13 July 1974
... The History Book on the shelf, It's Always Repeating Itself

The summer of '74 heralds a new start for Dave and Jenny, who this afternoon made a public display of their love for one another and finally, after years of living in sin and producing two children, tied the knot. The ceremony was a quiet, family only affair at the Registry Office near to their house. The evening party at the Belvoir Hotel was expected to be somewhat louder with generally a lot more drunkenness and vomiting.

It's eight o'clock and already I've met family members I'd all but forgotten about, like Auntie Jane and Uncle Bob from Coventry, with my six-month old cousin in tow. It seems that Auntie Jane was expecting a girl and poor little Adrian is still wearing the huge supply of pink clothes bought for him before the birth. Alarmingly, Uncle Bob doesn't seem to have a problem with this right now, but will happily throw my cousin out into the street in seventeen years time when Adrian asks for a sex change.

I've also been introduced to my grandparents on my father's side, which was nice. My grandfather seems to have hardly changed in thirty years and it turns out my grandmother has actually been wearing unfashionable old-women's clothes since she was in her forties. And I finally got to meet my mother's parents too, Keith and Louise, who both died when I was way too young to remember much about them.

Right now, Dave is doing the rounds, saying 'hi' and 'thanks for the presents' to all the guests. It's a busy day for him, lots of people around, guests constantly moving about and shifting around. He probably doesn't even notice that his new bride and his best man are missing.

Right now, Jenny and me are on my bed in the hotel room I'm staying in overnight. She's supposed to be in the next room, changing out of her wedding dress and into some evening clothes, but she only managed to get half way through before I arrived and distracted her.

Most of the time, particularly the times when I'm drunk, I don't even think about Jenny being my mother. I've known her as a real person for four years now, someone with hopes and dreams, someone who talks to me and confides in me, someone who actually needs me. She's so far beyond the role of parent that it doesn't even warrant a guilty conscience anymore. Jenny is twenty-five years old now, much younger than I am and more beautiful than any of my hazy memories gave her credit for. She may be married to Dave, but I know that in around five years time she'll walk out and leave him and all of today's vows and promises will count for nothing. I know all this. For me it's history. I'm not doing anything to Dave's marriage that he won't do himself given time.

Jenny slowly shifts and right now, lying here with her on the bed, I can't even remember a time when doing all this actually felt wrong. She sits up, swings her legs to the floor, picks up the rest of her wedding dress and heads back to her room through the adjoining door.

"I'll meet you downstairs." I call after her. "I'll try and keep Dave busy until you get changed."

She pulls on a pair of jeans and stands in the doorway, topless and so incredibly attractive. "I won't leave him, you know." She tells me this as she kisses me hard on the mouth. And although I know this is only misguided optimism on her part, there's nothing much I can say.

Back at the bar I hand Dave a pint and make out that I've just spent an unholy twenty-five minutes in the toilet battling against the effects of last night's stag night Madras. Dave is thoroughly drunk and telling a crowd of assorted friends and family some joke about the three-day week which I join too late to understand but laugh along with anyway.

"So, David," slurs Uncle Bob, who for no readily explainable reason is drinking something blue with an umbrella in it. "Why'd you finally decide to get hitched? Getting scared someone would take your lovely wife away from you?"

"Well, I've had some time to think lately, Robert, and I'm not getting any younger and it just seemed like the right thing to do. You have to grow up and get responsible sooner or later."

"That's right! My little brother here is a first class example of our prison reform system, isn't that right? I always wondered why you never let anyone visit you. I suppose you were having too much trouble sitting down? And what happened to that ridiculous hat you used to wear? I always thought you'd be buried in that bloody thing!"

And Uncle Bob lets out a forced, drunken laugh and looks to see if anyone's going to back him up.

Dave casts his eyes heavenward. As far as I know my dad and his brother never really saw eye to eye on anything and have barely even spoken to each other since the sixties. Something very hush-hush went on, possibly involving my dad and my Auntie Jane. Like Dave's spell in prison, that bit of information has been carefully excised from the family history.

"I outgrew the hat, that's all. So how's Jane these days, Robert? Still as ravishing as ever?" And Dave looks around for her in an almost pantomime style whilst Uncle Bob starts going a nasty shade of crimson. The rest of the crowd shuffles a little uneasily as Dave leans over and whispers something in Bob's ear and then, smiling and pleased with himself, steps back.

Bob just loses it. The DJ, sensing something more exciting is kicking off, cuts the volume to his fourth ABBA track of the evening and in the sudden silence there's a glass hitting the floor, fists flying, Bob being held back and Dave laughing. Eventually, Bob calms down enough to start swearing and all eyes are turned on him as he holds a handkerchief to his bloody nose and casually threatens to slice Dave into a million pieces.

Dave doesn't even flinch. He just stands there, straightens his white carnation button-hole and says loud and clear for the benefit of the guests at the back of the room, "All I asked was, 'does Jane still like it up the arse?' A simple yes or no would have sufficed."

The silence is broken by the sound of Auntie Jane dropping her drink onto the dance floor and the DJ desperately starts playing *Stuck in the Middle with You* which seems oddly appropriate and almost premeditated.

The whole thing is being calmed down and moved along by the less drunk guests but is still missing the final punctuation which Dave supplies by once again punching Bob squarely in the face before going over to start chatting with Auntie Jane.

And as Bob is half-carried to the toilets I smell something familiar through the heavy cloud of cigar smoke and turn to see Jenny at my side, now dressed casually in jeans and a pullover. "He only invited Bob to keep his mother happy," she says. "And I suppose I'll be the one that spends the rest of the night smoothing things over. You know, the funny thing is that Dave and Jane never actually did anything, but for some reason Dave wants Bob to believe that they had this really dirty affair."

"There's a lot of it about." I say and wander over with Jenny to find Steve who apparently has various illegal substances that might make the rest of the evening flow a little faster.

By 9.15 the DJ seems to have lost the party spirit and has filled the evening with a run of Beatles tracks, moving almost seamlessly from *Eleanor Rigby*, through *The Long and Winding Road*, and finally ending up with *She's leaving Home*. It's like he's playing all the hits from *'The Worst Feel Good Party Album in the World – Ever – Volume Two'* and I find myself wondering where the hell he gets his recommendations from. Still, the kids are enjoying it and are making the most of staying up way past their bedtimes whilst the adults get pissed, smoke big fat cigars and generally eat themselves stupid on a mix of chicken vol-au-vents and spam sandwiches.

Dave and Jenny are dancing together and I'm so very nearly unconscious with the drink and drugs that for once I don't care that she isn't really mine. Somehow I repress the urge to stand on the DJ's stage, grab a microphone and tell these people a few home truths. In my head, I'm already striding up there and, mike in hand, it all just got bloody brilliant.

"Ladies and gentlemen, boys and girls, allow me a few minutes if you would to say a few words before we get to the last dance and all you dads out there get your final opportunity of the night to grope at the bridesmaids. I would like to point out though that some of these girls are only just into their teens, but I know that won't bother you too much, eh Uncle Jim? But don't worry, mate, it'll 1984 before they find enough evidence to convict you so you've got another ten years of ruining young girls' lives ahead of you yet.

"Now then, let me run down my list of people I have to give a special mention to. There's Bob and Jane, obviously, who have already helped make the evening such a special occasion in everyone's memories. Bob, of course thinks that my Dad and his missus got up to something, which is apparently wrong, but Jane does in fact get pregnant in a few years, so congratulations, Bob. I hear that every so often it's perfectly normal for two white parents to give birth to a half-African baby. Cheers!

"Next up is Auntie Phyllis who helped with the decorations today. Lovely job done there, Phyllis. Who'd have thought you have a secret drink problem and in 1990 manage to get yourself arrested for public indecency? And there's no need to worry about your husband being able to look after himself whilst you're doing three months in the clink. By the time you get out Gordon will be getting all his hot dinners prepared by Maggie from number thirty-three, if you get my drift.

"And last, but by no means least, a big thank-you to my mum, Jenny, who I've been secretly screwing behind Dave's back for the last two years and who will bugger off in another five with no explanation, leaving a broken family to pick up the pieces. You're a real work of art, Mum, a fantastic shag with a gorgeous pair of tits and I love you!"

That's how it all goes in my head.

It would be like shooting fish in a barrel. So many lives, so many secrets. For just one night they could all be out in the open, the future laid bare for all to see.

In reality I sit on the sidelines and watch the woman I love dance her way to midnight with her new husband. Through the window I see Uncle Bob and Auntie Jane out in the car park letting down the tyres on Dave's car.

They do say that there's nothing quite like family.

1974 – 1975

Following America's withdrawal from Vietnam, the war finally comes to an end in April 1975 when the North Vietnamese forces storm and occupy Saigon, forming a single, unified communist country.

During eighteen years of open conflict, the American War, as it was known to the Vietnamese, cost the lives of some fifty-eight thousand American soldiers, an average of nine fatalities each day. The casualty numbers for America's allies, Australia, New Zealand, Thailand and the Philippines are rarely reported upon.

The combined Vietnamese losses during the same period amounted to over two million soldiers and somewhere between two and four million civilians, outnumbering the American dead by over eighty to one.

The American involvement in Vietnam left the country in exactly the same state it would have been in had they never interfered. Which all seems a little unfortunate for around five million Vietnamese citizens who didn't survive long enough to see the end of the war.

11 August 1975
... It's Just Your Jive Talkin'

"When I first arrived in the past I really thought I'd got it made. I mean, what couldn't I do given my knowledge of the future? The moneymaking opportunities would be endless!"

The bloke in the pub is nodding along enthusiastically as he patiently listens to my outrageous story. I've never met him before but he's some foreign guy on holiday and his name's John something-or-other and he's drawn the short straw on this, the fifth anniversary of my arrival in the past. I'm drunk and babbling, but he really doesn't seem to care. He even buys more than his fair share of the drinks.

"The first six months I was here, I sent letters to all kinds of people explaining the benefits of Compact Disks, affordable personal computers, mobile phones and the internet. I was laughed out of town on every occasion. I mean, what kind of weirdo would come up with the idea of everyone in the world having their own high-tech computing machine that was connected to this massive world-wide network which allowed instant communication with people wherever they were in the world? Having been here for five years, it now seems pretty bloody farfetched to me. I mean, for God's sake, how many people do you know who even own a video recorder?"

And he's still nodding away, chuckling to himself, occasionally coming out with phrases like, "Computers, dude. Way of the future." He sounds American, or possibly from New Zealand, I'm not all that good at recognising accents.

"No, I was ignored and laughed at, though I'm sure some of the companies stole my ideas. I just found that nothing I did was actually making any difference to the world, that I couldn't really change anything that mattered. I was forced to settle down and live life like a spectator. I got a job selling stationery to large companies which pays my rent and leaves me a bit aside to invest in the futures market. Believe me, mate, if you want to make a bit of money put it in shares. Pocket calculators and digital watches are going to be big!"

John excuses himself and heads to the toilets, leaving me thinking that the money I make from investing is still not that great. I should really know more than I do about the seventies. It's like I've been dumped in the past with half my memory erased. For all I know, that's exactly what *has* happened.

I drain the last of my beer and pick up two new pints from the bar, handing over a couple of pound notes and still getting change. Another quirk of the past is how it took me hardly any time at all to get used to the prices, how it just all seemed to slot together, everything becoming second nature to me. Hardly like living in the past at all.

As I sit back down at the table and wait for John to come back, I consider, not for the first time this year, that I'm fast approaching my forty-first birthday. If I'd stayed where I should have been it would be 2011 by now and who knows what I'd be getting up to? Probably living it up with my futuristic, personal cyborg-girlfriend. I'd probably have moved on from Cassie and screwed up a few more lives and I'm sure no one back there misses me. I'm probably better off here in the past where I don't seem able to do too much and can be content with getting on with the average things in life like sleeping with my own mother.

John drops back down beside me and thanks me for the beer.

"So what do you think people will be doing in thirty-six years time?" I casually ask him.

He seems to think this is funny in some way. Keeps sniggering to himself.

"That Vietnam War thing that everyone has been so wound up about these last few years, well that's nothing. Thirty-odd years from now people are heading to the worst war in history. America will have spent so much time interfering with the rest of the world that it ignores its problems at home. There's a civil war, things get pretty bad and the goddam Russians of all people have to step in to sort it out! It's World War Three, my friend. Three billion people killed. America destroyed. Most of Europe wiped off the map."

Now it's my turn to nod sagely. "That's a fairly pessimistic view of things. You know, I probably shouldn't say these things, but the world does finally get its act together. On the whole, things get sorted out and the cold war only goes on until the nineties. Things do improve!"

"You're so wrong, my young, drunken, idealistic friend! I've seen what happens!"

I get the sudden sinking feeling that I'm sitting in the pub talking to yet another mad man. "You've seen the future?"

And he gets all conspiratorial, speaking in quiet, low whispers. "It's all top secret, but I'm on a mission for the US government. I've been sent back in time to collect a certain item that we need to clear up a computer bug. I'm from the year 2036."

"Right. Okay, John. That's just funky." This is bordering on the comical, though it occurs to me that it's also ironic that this brain-case is spouting his nonsense to someone who actually is from the future. "So what else do you know about the future? Who's President of America in 2036?"

"No-one you've ever heard of."

"That's handy. What's your time machine look like?"

"It's a black box with some switches and lights on it. I've got it housed in a '66 Chevy truck."

"And you've come back to 1975 for what?"

"That's classified intel, Jay. Government business. All incredibly hush-hush."

I'm nodding happily. "So you've come back what, sixty-one years in time, in a car from nowadays, from a future you can't really describe to me because I have no frame of reference, to get hold of something you can't tell me about?"

He nods. "Put like that, I guess it does sound a bit ... well, shoddy."

"Not to mention a bit crap. Want to show me your car?"

"I can't. It's classified. Sorry."

It hardly seems worth pursuing this, but I plough forward.

"Do you have anything from the future with you? Anything that can back up your story? Money? Your birth certificate? Signed mission orders given to you by the mystery President?"

John holds up his hands. "All right, okay! I have nothing. That doesn't make me any more of a liar than you, friend."

"But I really am from the future! I have proof!"

"So show me."

"It's classified." I sit back smugly, give him a few seconds to gather his wits and then, making sure no one in the pub is watching, fish my most prized possession out from around my neck.

Holding onto the chain, I lay the coin in his hand. "You're the first person I've ever shown this to. And I'm probably off my head for doing it, but this is the only thing I had on me when I woke up in 1970. It's a 2003 one pound coin, minted by the Bank of England and the only remaining link to my future."

"Wow! You actually went to the trouble of getting a future-coin made up to prove your story! I'm impressed!" He's trying for sarcasm in that American, I-haven't-got-a-clue-what-sarcasm-is, way but I can tell that deep down he really is impressed. "I can see I've met my match." He looks at his watch hurriedly. "Well, I'm sorry, Jay, but I really do have to be going. I have a future civilisation to save."

"Okay, John. You take care of yourself. And keep the timeline intact for me, all right? I'd like to think I've got a future of my own to go back to one day."

He winks at me and leans over the table. "Look, I'm stopping off on my way home to see my family in the year 2000. I could give you a lift if you like?"

I consider the pros and cons of getting into a truck to nowhere with an unbalanced psychopath and decide on staying in the seventies for the time being. "It's okay, John, I've still got things to do here, and I'm sure you have some classified rules about taking passengers along with you. But you have fun without me."

He pulls a notepad and a pen out of his jacket, scribbles something down, folds it and pushes it into my shirt pocket. "If you make it to 2000, look out for me. I'll be there for a while."

And he winks at me again like a pissed-up weirdo with a nervous tic and staggers drunkenly from the pub, leaving me with a strange, hollow feeling in my stomach, like I just missed something big.

I would have thought that after actually confessing to someone that I'm from the future I'd finally feel some sort of cathartic relief, but there's nothing. Perhaps next time I should pick someone a little less insane to be my confidant.

I finish off my pint and grab my coat for the journey home. Remembering the scrap of paper he gave me, I pull it out and unfold it, expecting some crazy mental-patient punch line. Right there, in front of my eyes, are the words:

Sept 11 2001- Twin Towers Fall

I quietly fold the note back up and push it back into my pocket, suddenly aware that my world doesn't seem quite as secure as did an hour ago.

1975 – 1976

By the mid-seventies the world of computing was heading forward in leaps and bounds and in late 1975 America unveiled their latest top-secret development, the first prototype 'NERD'.

The NERD, (or Neurologically Enhanced Research and Development), program had begun back in the fifties when genetic scientists managed to impregnate a woman with an artificially enhanced embryo. Rumours concerning the birth rocked the world of science and today it is generally believed that the foetus contained either alien DNA from Roswell or was in some way connected to the super-soldier project that created Captain America. Whatever the source, the experiment was a success and young Billy, the first 'Enhanced Human', was born.

For years Billy rarely left his bedroom, choosing to spend his hours tinkering with electronics and entering the number five million, three hundred and eighteen thousand and eight into his shiny new pocket calculator. It is believed that, upon entering puberty, Billy underwent a secondary mutation and in his new form found himself able to mentally process huge sums of information at unheard of speeds. His understanding of physics, electronics and mathematics were increased tenfold, whilst his understanding of girls was reduced to an almost non-existent level.

Curiously at this same time, he developed an uncontrollable addiction to the ladies underwear section of the Sears catalogue. But who cared? Billy knew that one day, with the powers he controlled, he was going to be rich and famous.

All of which is all very interesting, and has nothing whatsoever to with the rise of Bill Gates, who emerged from college in the mid-seventies and formed the Microsoft Corporation.

17 September 1976
... Don't Fear the Reaper

Since this was the seventies and Internet research was pretty much restricted to the United States military, I had no success at all in tracking down' John' after our meeting in the pub. All I had to go on was his description, first name and the less tangible fact that he may be driving a time machine disguised as a Chevy truck. I spoke to the people in the pub that evening who vaguely remembered me speaking to someone who may have been a bloke, possibly a 'mannish girl' and in desperation I filed a complaint with the police that I'd been mugged by an American in a battered leather flying jacket in the hope that they'd keep an eye out for him.

A month later there was surprisingly little progress and I'd settled back down to my seventies life, content in my job selling biros, rulers and notepads to the businesses of the developing world. I even managed to keep an occasional eye on the little Julian who was now at that that awkward first-years-in-school age.

Jenny was finding her life pretty busy these days with two kids and a husband to look after and part of me really hoped that she'd just stop messing around with me behind Dave' s back and just sort her life out. But she still found time to get together with me each week and, after increasingly mechanical sex, she would moan to me that Dave was no longer the person she'd fallen in love with. She stayed with him for the kids, did the right thing for the kids, married him and played the dutiful wife for the kids. About six months ago she got drunk and told me she was going to leave Dave, Julian and Marie and run away with me. Fortunately she changed her mind pretty quickly when she sobered up. I could see where things were heading and it's all become a bit of a difficult time for me now. The guilt is beginning to increase again every time I look at Dave. Now, whenever I see him, I see the dad I knew from the future and I see the nagging doubt that was always present behind his eyes. For the past few years I've hidden from the approaching truth, but it really is beginning to look like it was me that destroyed their marriage.

And on the nights I'm not with Jenny, I tend to wind up drinking with Dave, listening to him telling me that his life's going downhill. He knows that he's losing her, that Jenny isn't really his anymore. One night he actually burst into tears with the realisation that he was being pushed aside and didn't know why and he couldn't figure out what he could do about it.

"People change," is all I could tell him. "I was married once. It lasted two years and left me homeless and broke. You still have her and you still have two great kids. You're still winning from where I'm sitting. You just need to make her feel special and wanted."

Which seemed to perk him up a little, but I knew that no matter how special and wanted he made her feel, eventually he was going to lose. If I was any kind of real friend, if I was any kind of real son, I'd stop shagging his wife and let them sort out their differences. But it's exactly that kind of behaviour that brought me to Phoenix Park in 2006. People can change, it seems. All except me who's apparently too stupid to see sense.

One way or another the next four years are shaping up to be hell for everyone concerned.

I'm sitting around my house, minding my own business, keeping out of trouble and being silently thankful that another week of drudgery has finished at Stationery HQ. I'm wondering how long it will be before my stock investments finally earn me enough for me to give up work when there's a knock at the front door.

I scribble down a few notes about the emerging computer industry noting that this coming year should see good investment opportunities in Microsoft, Apple and the US space programme, and head to the front door where I find Steve smiling at me from the porch with a thick file of papers in his arms.

"I'm glad you're back from work, mate, I've got something I want you to read!" And he bounds past me and into my front room.

"What's the hurry, Steve? Got plans to restart the Hendrix Revival?" Mercifully that particular movement had died a rather sudden death when two of its members were arrested in London and two of them vanished to Leeds. On a more serious point I did hear lately that Viv and Diane were now numbered among the ten most violent protesters currently active in the UK and a worrying thought occasionally crosses my mind that Pete must be over half way through his sentence now and could wangle an early parole anytime soon.

"Nothing of the sort, Jules, my man. I know you haven't seen much of me these past couple of months, but I've been busy!" He hands me the folder of papers.

I must admit that I hadn't really tried to get in touch with Steve for a month or two and just assumed that since everyone wasn't as close as they used to be that he was just spending time in his room getting up to whatever people do when they're nearing thirty and still living with their parents.

I open up the cover of the folder and there in neat black-typed script is a title:

The Godfather, Part Three - Fredo's Revenge

Inwardly, I'm in stitches, barely able to contain myself. On the outside I'm nodding seriously and rubbing my chin. "Oh, wow, Steve! You've written a screenplay! This must have taken you ages!"

"I'm going to send it to Coppola, you know, maybe get some feedback, hopefully get him to use it for his next film. Even if he doesn't like the whole script, I'm sure there are bits of it he could use."

I drop the papers onto the table beside my armchair, dangerously close to the wastepaper bin. "I'll get back to reading that in a minute. This sort of achievement deserves a drink! Want one?"

I head to the fridge and pull the door open, wondering if there's any way of getting out of this. I consider just leaving quietly by the back door, claiming a family emergency, but finally decide I have to face my demons so I grab us a can of beer each, head back to the living room and settle down in my armchair whilst Steve plonks himself down on the sofa. He's grinning like a loon and is clearly proud of his not inconsiderable three hundred page manuscript which I pick up again and start to absent-mindedly flick through. Somewhere around the middle I'm sure I spot the word 'zombie', but that can't be right.

"I got the idea last year when I saw Part Two and I got thinking that there were a few uncompleted storylines. I was left wondering what the hell happens to Michael now his family life has all but failed. What would happen to his children given that they have a gangster for a father? And most importantly for me, whatever happened to Fredo? Because we never actually see him getting killed, we just hear that shot and then he's lying down in the boat. What if he isn't actually dead? What if he waits patiently for years and when it's least expected, he starts up a series of revenge killings against his brother? I reckon that if I'm asking these questions, so are other *Godfather* fans around the world."

I feel like I've been nodding for ages by the time Steve finally finishes his speech and I force myself to stop before my neck starts to ache. "So you wrote all this in the last two months, eh? That is one enormous labour of love, Steve."

"I want you to be the first to read it. I know you're probably busy, but I need someone's opinion. I've put a synopsis at the back so you can get an idea of what's going on and give me an initial reaction."

Sure enough, the last three pages is an edited highlights account of the film, a cut-down version that may just get me out of reading the whole three hundred pages.

With mounting trepidation I give in to Steve's exuberance and start to run through the outline.

It is the future and many years have passed since the events of The Godfather, Part II. *Michael is now living out his old age in the Bahamas, trying to forget his violent past and concentrate on doing some good for the world with his remaining years. He spends a lot of time keeping a greenhouse filled with rare orchids and has a zoo filled with endangered species and orphans.*

He has also started a scientific foundation and throughout the nineteen eighties he has developed many things to help humanity. He has a team of top scientists gathered from all over the world who have provided him with a cure for many cancers, a cheap renewable energy source to replace petroleum, robots that can do jobs in places that humans can't work in and his latest invention, the flying car.

Unfortunately for Michael, someone has been using the Corleone Institute for their own ends, using the top-level scientists there to create new weapons; bombs controlled by intelligent computers, armies of zombie warriors and robot killing machines called Cybots.

Michael knows nothing of this to begin with, but starts to get suspicious when an explosion at the institute reveals a secret underground lab that no one knew existed.

Meanwhile, Michael's youngest daughter, Sicily, is elected the first female President of America and proclaims that during her first term in office she will outlaw all forms of terrorism including the Mafia. This news saddens Michael as he knows it will cause trouble for his son Anthony who now runs the Corleone family along more or less peaceful lines.

Anthony's business is predominantly concerned with casinos, but in the late eighties all forms of gambling are illegal and he knows that his sister will target him first to ensure that she is not seen to be showing favouritism to her brother. Add to this explosive situation the fact that Sicily and Anthony have not seen eye to eye since Anthony accidentally killed her pet puppy back when she was five and we have a king-size problem in the making.

Meanwhile the surviving members of Michael's old gang are being killed off one by one and Michael knows that whoever is responsible will be coming for him soon. He heads back to New York by flying car to team up with his son and get some answers.

A bloodbath ensues. Michael and Anthony wrongly assume that rival gang-boss, Alphonse Pelagio is responsible for the Corleone murders and in a gunfight scene lasting almost thirty minutes, some five hundred people are killed and a whole New York city block is reduced to rubble by giant Mafia robots.

Michael and Anthony are the only two left standing and, as a result of this action, Sicily Corleone implements marshal law and diverts all military resources at her disposal to the capture of her father and brother.

In a secret headquarters hidden in the Statue of Liberty, a wheezing old man sits in the half-dark and laughs at how well his plan is progressing. By his side is Michael's ex-wife, Kay, gloating along with him at how their revenge on the whole Corleone family is almost complete. The man stands, revealing a half-man, half machine construct, a cybot-enhanced Fredo Corleone.

He kisses his partner in crime, Kay and proclaims that it is time for the final confrontation.

In a dream Michael is visited by his father, Vito, who explains to his son in mumbled tones that all things are not yet lost and that there is one person he needs to find to stop the situation getting any worse. 'You have to make him an offer he cannot refuse' the ghost says, stroking a fat white cat. Michael knows to whom the Don is referring and he wakes up, drenched in sweat, sitting bolt upright in bed and shouting out the name of his brother, Fredo.

Michael and Anthony set up a rooftop meeting with Sicily atop the Corleone Institute building, now the tallest building in New York. They all arrive and Michael begins explaining that he knows who is causing the trouble for the family. Unwilling to believe that her father is using the memory of poor old Uncle Fredo as a scapegoat, Sicily calls in an air strike, knowing that although she will die, she will take the last of the Corleone family with her and live in history as the President who finally wiped out the gangster threat. With the planes on the way, Fredo arrives in a flying car and confronts Michael.

All these years, Fredo explains, he has waited. He has used Michael's institute to repair and enhance his body, kept himself alive long enough to get his revenge. He hates Michael and his family and has created an army of robot zombies armed with laser guns to take over the world.

As the air strike arrives and the missiles are fired at the roof, Fredo uses a jet pack to escape, laughing as his brother, his nephew and his niece are destroyed in a massive fireball of fiery death.

As the flames die down the scene cuts to Fredo and Kay in their Statue of Liberty lair, watching huge television screens on which he can see his undead robots marching on Washington, Moscow, London and Paris. Everything they meet is cut down by their laser death-rays and, as the bodies fall, the film fades to black and all we hear is the wheezing laughter of Fredo, Godfather of the World.

I close the ring-binder containing Steve's masterpiece and resume my nodding. I can tell he's just sitting there, waiting for some sort of feedback on the two months he's spent locked in his room with a typewriter. .

"Can I be brutally honest?" I ask.

"I wouldn't want anything else!"

I stand figuratively at the junction of two roads. To my left lies the narrow path of truth and righteousness, a difficult, barren passage, beset on both sides by the thorny briars of evil and darkness. To my right is the wide easy road of lies and deception filled with bars, night clubs, brothels and rock music. And I think to myself, what would Jesus do in this situation?

"It's fabulous!" I tell him, figuring that Jesus would probably take the wide, easy path after all those times he spent in the briar-filled wilderness. "I'm not sure that the special effects are going to be easily attainable, I mean, this is more than just a plastic shark here! This is laser guns! This is flying cars! It's exactly what the public are going to need in 1977."

Steve is quite clearly overcome with my appraisal of his work.

Almost in tears, in fact.

"If I had to make some suggestions, I'd include a couple of Popes and a sung version of the Godfather Theme with lyrics, but other than that, it's spot on."

I stand up and hand the folder to Steve. "I'd love to go through the whole thing, mate, but I'm going away this weekend and I'm barely going to have time to read anything, plus I think you should get this thing copied up and sent out to Coppola whilst it's still hot."

"You're sure?"

"Positive. This thing is years ahead of its time."

I make a mental note to record this day for posterity and, as I jostle Steve bodily out of the front door, reflect on how much better the real *Godfather, Part Three* suddenly seems to have become.

1976 – 1977

Upon entry to the United States of America, immigrants and visitors alike will be stunned by the majesty and iconic power of the great, green Statue of Liberty. Since 1903 a plaque on the museum wall has contained the now famous poem:

Give me your tired, your poor,
Your huddled masses yearning to breathe free,
The wretched refuse of your teeming shore,
Send these, the homeless, tempest-tost to me,
I lift my lamp beside the golden door!
But don't dare send any disgusting gays,
Or we'll torture them for their deviant ways!

With all due respect to the poem's writer, Emma Lazarus, the last two lines have been added to The New Colossus so as to update it with the spirit of '77 and help to show how enlightened the world had become since the early nineteen hundreds.

Early in 1977, Dade County in Florida showed itself to be progressive and forward thinking and passed a law prohibiting discrimination on the grounds of sexual orientation. To save mankind from such insane policies, Anita Bryant, a Southern Baptist from Oklahoma, a one-time singer and alleged orange juice addict, lobbied to get the law repealed and in June 1977 the edict was retracted with a majority of 69%. Bryant used cleverly thought-out logic in her campaign such as the immortal line; "If gays are granted rights, next we'll have to give rights to prostitutes and to people who sleep with St. Bernards and to nail-biters."

People were persecuted and in at least one incident, brutally stabbed to death in the name of democracy. Strangely, despite the heightened levels of civil unrest being caused, it would remain perfectly lawful to discriminate against homosexuals in Dade County until 1998.

Thankfully Ms Bryant now has a string of failed businesses, bankruptcies and doomed relationships to look back on and her singing career has also failed to work out quite the way she intended.

So maybe there is a God, after all.

Elsewhere, Elvis 'The King' Presley dies, finally ending the influence of the monarchy in America and handing full decision-making authority over to the Senate.

And finally, the Space Shuttle conducts its first test flight and everyone on Earth is wondering where the Space Race is going to take them next. On a clear night folks could be seen staring up at the stars and squinting, and, if they looked really, really hard, they could just make out the light blue lettering hovering in the sky:

A long time ago, in a galaxy far, far, away...

17 August 1977
... No Future

This was the year I was really waiting for. My memory of events is hazy at best and, truth be told, I'd have difficulty telling you which year, let alone which month or day, any particular event happened. Troops leaving Vietnam, the first mobile phone call, the first computer or the invention of the CD were all pretty much indistinct events that happened sometime in the past, though I could probably, if pushed, give you a decade.

But 1977, was *the* year! This was the release of Star Wars! Memories of long queues, sitting impatiently through adverts and cartoons before finally watching as Luke flies his X-Wing down the Death Star trench. Of course, by the time I was in my thirties, I'd seen the film and its sequels so often that I knew almost every line and yet I still loved every minute of it. This time around I took little Julian and Marie to see it and experienced again the whole extravaganza of one of the first big science fiction blockbusters. Everything that came after this would be nothing more than a pale imitation.

Julian was predictably amazed by the whole thing. Marie, I think, found it a bit far-fetched, but she's only four years old and slept through most of it, so I'm not sure her opinion really counts. Granted, back in the future she will still berate my obsessive fan-boy mentality, never missing a chance to point out the sadness of my taste in films, and letting her see me cheer as the opening credits rolled probably didn't help the situation in the slightest.

For me it was pure heaven. To sit in a cinema full of people seeing the Death Star for the first time is an experience I never expected to relive. This is what being in the past is all about, this is the sort of thing that makes up for missing out on the twenty-first century. Back in March I sent a birthday card to the young Ewan McGregor which said inside, 'To my second favourite Jedi, best wishes and may the Force be with you - always.' Which will confuse the hell out of him for years.

But as always, you wait years for a film to come along and then it's all over and life goes on as normal. A couple of weeks after Star Wars it was all the pomp and circumstance of the great Silver Jubilee celebrations which, considering it was only about ten years ago that I had to endure the Golden Jubilee, I could have done without.

But oh, what a time! What a spirit of community! What a lot of street parties! Dave, Jenny, the kids and me went to one in the street next to where I grew up. I remember it well from when I was a child, an overpowering memory of having all the sandwiches and cakes you could eat, enough to make you sick in fact. There was red, white and blue bunting, sausages on sticks, cheese and pineapple on sticks, jam tarts - on sticks, mugs and plates with the Queen's face on them and a brass band which predictably played the National Anthem, and less predictably the theme from *Jaws*, the theme from *M*A *S*H* and the theme from *Star Wars*. There was dancing, singing, much, much drinking, and at some point little Julian getting slapped about by Jenny for peeing in the bushes of Mrs Wilberforce's garden.

We bailed out before the party ended and headed back to put little Julian and Marie to bed. To be honest there was only so much of that *'Festival of Britain'* spirit I could take. So we nipped back round the corner into the house and whilst Jenny put the kids to sleep, me and Dave grabbed some more beers and finally caught our breath for what seemed like the first time that day. Maybe it was a combination of the beer and the exhaustion, but, as I pulled a couple of purloined cheese and onion sandwiches from my jacket pockets, I found myself finally asking some things that had worried me for ages.

"So, Dave, I've wanted to ask you some things for ages now and, well, it's been a few years and, well, just what did happen to you when you were in prison?"

Dave just glared at me uncomfortably and I felt like now would be a good time for the armchair to swallow me whole and spit me out sometime next week, preferably when Dave wasn't home.

"Feel free to tell me to bugger-off, but it's been like, what, five years? You changed, man. Everyone wanted to see you, let you know that we were there for you. Everyone waited, especially Jenny, and when you finally came out of there you acted like the old days never existed. What happened to you? Where's that Dennis Hopper character everyone used to love? Where, for fuck's sake, is the hat?"

He poured his beer from the can into a glass and sat staring at the bubbles long and hard before finally saying, "Just leave it, okay?"

I should have accepted his wishes on this, but something in me wouldn't let go. It was almost like I wanted him to be angry, I wanted something inside him to snap. I wanted something to make him care enough to realise that his wife was having an affair.

"You could at least tell me what happened to the hat!"

He put his beer down on the table with a bit more force than I expected. "Look. It was prison. I had a lot of time on my hands. A lot of thinking time. I got to think particularly about what I was doing with the whole Easy Rider act. And I didn't want people to see me because I was ashamed, all right? I was embarrassed because I wound up in prison because I thought there was some government conspiracy killing off our heroes. I thought decimal currency was a covert means of controlling the population. I was embarrassed because I couldn't be there to see my son's first steps, I couldn't even look after my own family! I missed out on Julian's first words because I was stupid and fucked up."

He was barely looking at me, just staring into the fireplace, his shoulders shaking. I let him recover from his quiet outburst, hoping it wasn't loud enough to bring Jenny downstairs before he finished telling me his story. I wanted to hear the things my dad would never tell me.

"I didn't find God," he continued. "I didn't convert to Buddhism, I wasn't shagged in the showers or initiated into a cult of Manson worshippers. I was just ... embarrassed."

The poor guy. In my old life I never had any idea that this had happened. No one had ever mentioned my dad going to prison. And all I could think of as I sat there with him was the night when he was a few months into his sentence and me and Jenny ended up in bed together for the first time. Dave finally spills his guts about his time away, letting out all his repressed memories and stuff he'd never even spoken to Jenny about, and all that goes through my mind are images of his wife on my bed, the curve of her breasts, the toned muscles in her stomach, her long slender legs, the way a sunbeam from the window would suddenly highlight the gold in her hair. Suddenly, I felt more uncomfortable than I'd been in years.

"So what happened to the hat?" I asked again, hoping to clear my head and lighten things up.

For the first time in years, Dave seemed genuinely emotional.

"They took it off me when I went inside. When I was ready to leave, someone had apparently 'lost it'. It didn't seem that important anymore. I was convinced that I was a new man, with a new road to walk with Jenny and my son. I had to be the man of the house and there was no room in there for conspiracy theories or dressing like film stars." He looked over at me, sadness covering his face, "I do miss that hat though, Jay."

I nodded, smiling at this tiny glimpse of the old Dave, as Jenny wandered into the room from upstairs and kissed Dave on the forehead. With yet more guilt building up inside me, I made my excuses and headed home.

And then here we are again, it's August already and I'm in bed with Jenny and I'm trying to concentrate on what she's saying, but my mind keeps drifting to other things. I'm thinking that Marc Bolan has died in a car crash, I'm thinking that Elvis ate one too many burgers. I'm thinking that I already know Charlie Chaplin will die on Christmas Day. And I feel trapped in the past and yet all the time that same past is slipping away, pushing me forward and there's nothing I can do about it.

For the millionth time it hits me that nothing I'm doing in the past is making a blind bit of difference. People are still dying, news is still happening and my being here is changing nothing at all.

And Jenny stops saying whatever it was she was saying and lays a delicate hand on my shoulder.

"What's wrong? You look like you're somewhere else today."

"I know."

Just what do you do when you eventually realise that fate really does exist? What are you supposed to do with your life when you know that nothing you say or do will change a single thing? Whatever I say to my younger self will fall on deaf ears, if I bought a gun and tried to kill someone who was alive in my time, something would happen to stop me. When I try to sell the technological secrets of the future I'm labelled a fraud or a madman. Everyone has been born, lived and died in exactly the way they should have done. Nothing I do will ever change the future.

It's so clear now.

I know that in April 1979 my mother will leave my father. She packs a bag whilst he's at the pub and disappears from his life forever. Neither my dad, or my sister or any friends of the family will ever hear from her again.

"I love you, Jen." I tell her, not for the first time.

"I love you, too." Her voice is so soft, so quiet. She's never told me that before.

And there, lying in bed with Jenny, I finally understand that it will me that she leaves my father for. In one year and eight months it will be me that destroys my father's life. It will be me that forces my younger self to grow up without a mother. Everything will be down to me. Maybe it always was.

I hug her to me as tight as I can and screw my eyes shut, wishing for sleep to take me away from reality and knowing that by the time I wake up, she'll be gone.

1977 – 1978

It's another year of airplane disasters, disintegrating space stations, terrorist bombers and no less than three Popes holding the office in as many months. Yet as bad as the world seems to be, things get worse still when everyone finds out that there's a poisonous ozone layer circling the planet and, even more worryingly, there are holes in it, allowing things like radiation and aliens easy access to the Earth's population.

Scientists work hard at finding a solution, but to their dismay find that it's already too late. Radiation coming through the ozone holes has caused outbreaks of the deadly 'Saturday Night' fever throughout the world. Much of the population is affected, though young and impressionable males seem to show the most symptoms.

When the SNF virus first strikes the patient suffers few ill effects, but over time they lose the capacity to properly co-ordinate their clothing, later resulting in a complete inability to fasten up a shirt past the bottom three buttons. Strangely, the victim's sense of rhythm and hand-eye coordination actually improves.

No cure has ever been found, though the disease seems to have died out naturally sometime in the early eighties. Occasional new cases of SNF are reported, though they are thankfully localised and relatively short-lived.

Scientists are also still working on a cure for the few remaining cases of Coleman's disorder, which was also first reported in 1978. With symptoms similar to Tourette syndrome, these victims would wander the streets of major cities yelling "What you talkin' 'bout, Willis" at total strangers.

One in ten thousand people's lives are still ruined by Coleman's disorder each year. Please give generously.

16 October 1978
... I Can't Seem to Face Up to the Facts

It seems like I've barely slept for the last year. Every time I close my eyes I find myself dreaming about things I'd rather ignore. I have dreams where Dave finds out I've been sleeping with Jenny, I have nightmares where Jenny leaves me for Dave, and the worst ones of all are where I dream that I've woken up back in my own time and it's 2006 and none of this has happened, that meeting Jenny was all just a figment of my fevered imagination and once again I'm all alone.

All that my dreams seem to be telling me is that, one way or another, I'm soon going to lose the woman I love. And if that's all they have to tell me, then I think I'd rather not listen.

So tonight, like most nights, I'm lying in bed, staring at the ceiling in the pale light that's filtering through the curtains, waiting for sleep to finally pull me under. There's nothing to do at three in the morning. No twenty-four hour television, no computers, no internet. And the radio plays the same night-time broadcasting crap back in 1978 as it did in 2006.

Around my neck I can feel the weight of the pound coin that I've carried with me for the past eight years, the little memorial of where I'm from. Jenny once asked me what it was and I told her it was a just prop I'd bought from a science fiction movie where a bloke travels to a future where they don't use paper money anymore.

"It's supposed to have actually been held by Marlon Brando." I told her.

And something in her eyes replied, *you're such a liar*.

I lay in a too-warm bed, the covers pulled down to my waist, my arms stretched out to either side and suddenly I catch a scent on the air. I can't quite place it, but it's there, faintly alcoholic, the smell of whisky even though I haven't been drinking.

I close my eyes and try to concentrate, but get the stupid impression that I'm no longer alone. I try to ignore the chills down my spine, but have to open my eyes. There's a flash of blue in the corner of the room, by the wardrobe, a figure, a woman.

I sit bolt upright, staring, but it's gone. There's nothing there. Just the night playing tricks on the unbalanced nerves of a man who hasn't had enough sleep for months.

I lay back, my head falling into the pillows and the room suddenly feels way too cold.

I open my eyes again and squint as the early morning light rushes into my head and sends a knifelike pain slicing through my brain. Something isn't quite right. I'm hung over after a night without drinking, I'm wet through, still fully clothed and this isn't a bed I'm lying on. It's grass.

I sit up and my head gets a hundred times worse before it settles down to a quiet, throbbing nausea.

Looking around I can see I'm in a field and though it's clear skies now, it's been raining enough to have soaked me to the skin whilst I slept.

Cold and wet, I stand up realising that this is somehow August 1970.

It's day I arrived back in my own past. My clothes are the ones I was wearing that night at Phoenix Park. I don't bother to check, but in my pocket will be a single, 2003 minted, one pound coin.

There won't be a business park built on this site for years, but there's a road not far from the field that will take me back into town. I've been here before and know that I've got a long walk ahead of me in a pair of wet jeans. Fortunately, it's August and the summer heat is already building up nicely as I set off toward civilisation.

Almost instantly I'm in Nottingham city centre, confirming my suspicion that all this is just a dream and that in reality I'm still tucked up in bed, snoring soundly.

I'm standing in the Market Square, a slab-paved meeting point for all and sundry. My clothes have dried out on the walk into town though my hangover hasn't improved much. I remember all this from eight years ago. Standing around, watching blocky, old fashioned cars running around me, wondering at how strange the centre of town seems without its pedestrian zones, and how, even though the tram system is a relatively new addition to life in my time, the city now seems strange without it. Everything looks so much emptier.

And I'm here again looking at people dressed for Woodstock and watching shoppers running around, for once not all yelling into mobile phones or walking into things as they write text messages. There's not a Walkman or an iPod in sight and the internet enabled phone booths of the twenty-first century have been replaced by old-fashioned red boxes where a three minute call will cost less than a penny. I see the styling of shop signs, which even from my 1978 perspective seems old and dated and there isn't even a MacDonald's or a coffee shop to be seen.

This is all exactly as I remember it, standing here wondering what the hell I was going to do. I'm hungry, thirsty and in desperate need of some Paracetamol. I'm pretty sure that I smell quite bad too. I have an unusable pound coin in my pocket and am standing in the middle of a pre-decimalisation society with no one that I can call on for help.

I sit down on a low wall and watch the people go about their business. And here again, just like last time, I watch with fascination as a guy walks past me, pulls out his handkerchief and blows his nose. He walks away, mopping the sweat from his balding head, not realising that he's dropped his wallet. It's right there in front of me. I scoop it up, get to my feet and make it look as if I'm chasing after him, then duck into a shop doorway.

No one has noticed. No one comes after me. I pocket the wallet knowing from before that it contains enough cash for me to get a change of clothes, a decent meal and a train to Leicester where I can get a Bed and Breakfast for the night before heading out to find myself a job.

"You realise, of course that this position has very limited promotion prospects and that realistically you'll be doing work that you're very much overqualified for?"

This is Mr Spencer, my boss-to-be. He hasn't changed a bit in eight years, but he's right, the position is a total pile of crap. Be that as it may, it's money and it'll pay the rent and, since no one else has offered me a job today, I'll leap at this golden opportunity.

"That's okay. I really just need something that will keep me busy and I'm sure that my background working in an office and using office equipment will more than make up for my lack of sales experience. I'm very familiar with stationery."

Which is a fair approximation of the lame pitch I tried on at my interview to secure the job. Since this is all a dream I could presumably have told him that I just wanted an opportunity to sleep with his daughters and possibly his wife and I would have still got the position, but dreams tend to lead somewhere, so it's probably best not to stray too far from the original script.

Me and Mr Spencer shake hands, he gives me the job on the spot, my landlady at the B&B gives me a bit of leeway with the rent until payday and everything is working out very nicely indeed.

Reliving these things now, I'm amazed how it never occurred to me before that things could have gone very horribly wrong. At any number of turns I could have joined the hordes of the starving homeless. Still, I'd got a job, had a place to live with at least one meal a day thrown in and all I needed now was to track down my parents and start setting things straight with my younger self. What could possibly go wrong?

And in the blink of an eye I'm sitting at the bar ordering a pint of Guinness when Dave and Jenny come into the pub and Jenny goes and gets a table whilst Dave stands beside me, waiting patiently to be served.

I look at him, the first time I've seen him since arriving back here, and he looks back at me and nods. I point at him, trying to pull a thoughtful I'm-trying-to-remember-where-I-know-you-from face, hoping I don't just come across as some kind of freshly escaped psycho.

"Are you David Grant?" I ask, all innocent, like.

"Sure, man." Though he doesn't look so sure of this himself.

"I thought so! I wasn't certain with all the moustache and hat thing going on, but I thought it was you!" I hold out my hand enthusiastically. "I'm Julian! Julian... Grey!"

And Dave looks puzzled for some reason, not sure if he knows me or not.

"I was mates with your brother, Bernie at school! I used to come over and hang out at your place."

Dave starts nodding, hopefully mistaking me for any one of Uncle Bernie's mates who used to come over to hang out and listen to LPs. And the next thing you know we're all round the table chatting away like we're old friends, catching up on the past and getting hammered together.

Then, before I really know what's happening, Jenny is kissing me, her face pressed up against mine, and I know that things are getting out of hand but, as usual, I can't stop them. Dave is shouting something at me about keeping my hands off his girlfriend, but I'm only catching bits because the blood is roaring in my ears and all I can focus on is Jenny's tongue in my mouth and someone is tugging on my trouser leg and when I break away from her I see little Julian, about two feet tall standing there asking why I'm kissing his mummy, except it isn't little Julian, it's a two foot tall version of myself. And while I'm looking at myself and trying to stop him pulling at my leg, Dave just walks away and Jenny leans in close to my ear and whispers something that turns my blood to ice.

And I'm back in the dark, sitting bolt-upright, alone on my bed, drenched from head to foot in a cold sweat. And it's still three in the morning and there's no way I'm getting back to sleep.

In the pit of my stomach I can feel something hard and black and though I don't know what it is, I know it isn't pleasant.

I have a feeling that something very, very bad is about to happen.

1978 – 1979

The end of a decade and once more, testimony is generously given to a world gone mad.

In Guyana, cult leader and self-proclaimed messiah, Jim Jones, in his slave-labour community of Jonestown, asks his loyal followers to commit suicide, handing out cyanide-laced drinks to over a thousand people in his 'flock'. The poison was first given to the children and babies, many of them force-fed by syringe or tricked into drinking deadly fruit juice. Nine hundred and thirteen die, including two hundred and seventy-six children. Jones, who claimed to be the reincarnation of Christ, Buddha, and Lenin, was found shot in the head.

Elsewhere, in the early months of the United Nations' 'Year of the Child', around a hundred schoolchildren in the Central African Republic are killed during a demonstration over the compulsory wearing of expensive school uniforms. Many of those escaping the slaughter were arrested at the order of military leader, Jean-Bedel Bokassa.

And as the seventies ends amid all this insanity, the YMCA puts everything in perspective by suing the Village People because their hit disco song makes the organisation sound a little bit fruity.

On the plus side, following on from the Dade County gay rights debate of 1977, a nail-biting prostitute whose only client's were St.Bernards, was pleased to discover that her civil liberties remained intact and she was not facing either discrimination or persecution for the way she led her life.

29 April 1979
... Love is So Confusing

It was always 'soon' or 'maybe next week', it was always 'he needs me', and it was always 'I need to think about the kids'. It became alternately a standing joke and a cause for argument. In the end I knew that it was no good forcing the issue and it wouldn't be until April that Jenny would leave my father. The past month has been nothing short of a strain, expecting every day to be that day and being continuously put off, constantly having to wait.

I've lived for about two years with the knowledge that it would be me that my mother runs away with and that this is the reason why I'd been sent back to the past. I was to finally give meaning to both her life and mine. This had become my only certainty, the mantra I could use to keep me going each day.

And then yesterday everything crumbled to dust.

Over the last few weeks I've pushed her harder to leave Dave as each day in April passed and here, at the end, my frustration that I might now be left with nothing was making things even more difficult. I desperately needed to make things happen.

"But I love you, Jenny!" I told her for what seemed like the millionth time. "And you don't love Dave, you love me! I just can't take being your second choice anymore! If you truly love me, you'll end it. I'll take Dave to the pub tonight and while we're out, you can pack and go to my house. We'll leave when I get home and we'll be out of Leicester before Dave even knows you're missing." I could see the same old retorts forming on her lips and moved in first, the lies slipping out so easily. "The kids will be fine. When we're set up somewhere else we can send for them. We can let them know where we are. We can get custody. Judges always side with the mother in cases like these."

She sobbed and held me and I comforted her and told her that I had enough money put aside that we didn't need to worry about jobs for a while, we could just stay together and enjoy life. We'd head south, maybe to Cornwall, as far away as we could get from Dave without leaving the country.

She's thirty years old now and I've known her for almost ten years.

During that time I've barely looked at another woman. But, putting love and emotion to one side, for me this decision is just a matter of history, the way things were always destined to work out. For her it's the biggest thing she's ever done in her life, she's leaving behind her husband, her kids and everything she holds dear.

I felt like a complete bastard. I mean, how could I tell her that she'd never see her children again? It wasn't really going to do a lot to help my side of the argument.

"I'll get him drunk and be home by half past ten. Get to my house and have everything ready by ten o'clock to be on the safe side. I wouldn't want you bumping into him at a crucial moment." We kissed, we hugged, and I remember telling her as she left my house, "Everything will be fine. I love you so much."

And so, with everything planned out, I met Dave in the pub and whilst he got drunk, I took it steady and we both talked the usual, inconsequential pub talk about TV and football and I watched the hands of the clock above the bar tick by one painfully slow minute at a time.

By ten o'clock I was getting impatient. I went to the toilets more often than was strictly necessary, I was nervous and must have looked a wreck. At least Dave was too drunk to notice that I was almost counting off the seconds on my fingers.

Eventually, an eternity later, we left the pub and I walked Dave halfway home to the point where our paths separated. We shouted our goodbyes at each other in true drunken style and I headed to my place, completely unable to stop myself breaking into a run.

At the house all the lights were off and the front door still locked. I stupidly shouted out Jenny's name as I stood in my hallway, flicking the lights on and almost stumbling over the suitcases I'd packed earlier.

My stomach lurched and my legs gave out from under me as realisation hit. She wasn't there. She wasn't coming.

She'd changed her mind yet again.

Maybe I'd got it wrong. Perhaps I'd been living in a dream world and based everything on my hopeful certainty that she left Dave for me. With only two days left in April, and I'm certain it was April, it looks like it was probably me that forced her away. The choice I gave her was too much and she finally chose to go away alone.

It must have been ten or fifteen minutes later that I realised I was just curled up on the floor where I'd fallen, staring at the stitching on the corner of a suitcase just six inches from my head.

I eventually forced my legs and arms to work, climbed to my feet and made myself check every room. You know, just to be sure. But the house was predictably silent.

So I just sat there in my living room in the dark, the yellow streetlight illuminating the furniture and the life I was so ready to leave behind. And I drank whatever I could find and I waited and I stared at the clock and eventually, at somewhere around three in the morning, I managed to fall asleep.

And now today, the twenty-ninth, the phone at Dave and Jenny's house goes unanswered and I'm wandering through each of the rooms in my home like a ghost. It's just past midday and I've already drunk all the alcohol I can lay my hands on. I've smashed every mirror I've passed, sickened by the leering, dishevelled reflection each one contained. I've found every little gift, every knick-knack, every childish stuffed toy that she ever bought me and variously smashed, burned, ripped or drowned them.

It's strangely satisfying to watch the expression on a teddy bear's face as I hold it underwater, my hands wringing its soggy neck. And then, after doing the evil deed I spent ten minutes rolling on the bathroom floor, laughing at my attempts to take out everything on a cuddly toy. When that finished and the giggles became nothing but harsh, choked retching, I ripped off the bear's head and threw it at the window with all the force I could muster.

In the bedroom, the bed we shared over these last few years is tipped on its side and I'm about to go to work on the photo albums when I break down again and start sobbing uncontrollably. When I don't think things can get any worse, I remember that I've nothing left to drink.

If I want to drink more, then I have to go out. If I go out I'll find myself passing their house. And there it is. My decision, born out of necessity.

I'll confront my fears, the worry that has sat at the back of my mind since last night, the thought that she hasn't left at all, that my memory of events is faulty and that she's still here and she and Dave are staying together forever.

As I fell asleep last night I know a part of me was thinking that maybe this was how things should have worked out. Perhaps I'd got it all totally wrong. Maybe I was sent back in time to get them both to stay together, to give myself and my sister the upbringing and home life we never had. It would make a whole lot more sense that way. A new future for my family, bought at the cost of my own happiness.

If I ever want to sort this thing out then I'm going to need some more Scotch.

It takes me ten minutes to get to Dave and Jenny's house and though I'm still wearing yesterday's clothes and probably smell like I slept in a vat of mixed spirits, I don't want to waste any time. I should probably have phoned first, but since no one's answering it hardly seems to matter.

I knock on the door, almost hard enough to remove the green paintwork and wait for someone to answer. It occurs to me that since the curtains are closed they may still be in bed, or worse still, may have gone away for a while, leaving me with no easy ending to my sorry little plan.

I head round to the back and try to see what's going on through the kitchen window, but it's too dark inside and I can't make anything out clearly. My stomach dips suddenly as I wonder if Jenny has told Dave about me and her. It hadn't occurred to me before, but maybe the whole affair has been brought out into the open. Maybe Dave is after my blood.

More hesitantly, I knock on the kitchen window and, almost too quietly to be heard, call out, "Dave? Jenny? Anyone there?"

Their neighbour, Mrs Kennedy, a chain-smoking, mother-of-five that I've occasionally had half-intelligible conversations with, mostly about how much she'd love to sell her kids to couples who can't have children, sticks her head out of her back door.

"They're probably sleeping it off, love." She tells me, dropping a cigarette onto her patio and lighting up another in a fluid, well-practiced motion.

"What's that?"

"Hung over, I expect. They were having a right barney last night after he came back from the pub."

Apart from her obvious talents in the childbearing and smoking departments, Mrs Kennedy has a host of surveillance techniques that could at times rival those of the FBI. She could get more information from holding a glass to a wall than government operatives could manage with a truck full of bugging gear.

"The shouting woke up my youngest and the language, well, I've never heard the sort!"

I'm guessing she probably has, given the names I've heard her calling her children from time to time. And I'm about to give up and try them on the phone later when I catch someone lurking in the dark behind the kitchen door.

Still half-drunk, I begin battering the back door. "Dave? Dave, mate, it's Julian. Let me in!"

Still nothing.

"Come on, Dave, I can see you in there. We need to talk."

And slowly I see him through the frosted glass of the door, moving closer, undoing the lock. When he finally show's himself he looks terrible, still wearing last night's clothes and more drawn than a hangover should account for.

I'm not sure which route is best to take here so I go for mindless optimism mixed with concern and trust to luck that Jenny hasn't told him about her and me.

"Dave, you look awful, mate. What the hell's going on? Why haven't you been answering your phone?"

Without saying a word he just walks back through his kitchen to the living room, leaving the back door open in what I can only assume is an invitation.

I step through and close the door, blocking out the ever more interested face of Mrs Kennedy who will probably be finding herself a glass and an adjoining wall to ensure a ringside seat for whatever happens next.

Dave has slumped into his chair and is taking large gulps of, judging by the half empty bottles lying around, a concoction of vodka, gin, martini and, for some reason, strawberry Nesquik. This is not a good sign.

"What's happened, Dave? You look like crap and smell worse than I do. Where's Jenny?"

He snorts a laugh and says simply, "Gone."

My heart sinks that little bit more as the realisation that she's left me for the second time in my life hits me hard and fast. This really shouldn't be a surprise and I should probably feel sorrier for Dave, but since it's all sort of my fault anyway, I don't see how I can. I'll settle for feeling sorry for myself and mopping up the mess as best I can.

"Where are the kids, Dave? Has she taken them?"

I drop onto the sofa, almost as dazed as he is and I realise that, drunk as I am, I'm still madly in love with her and I'm not sure how long that feeling will take to lose.

Dave shakes his head. "I called my mother this morning. She's looking after them for a few days while I get myself sorted out."

I suppose, if I still feel like leaving Leicester, I could try to track her down, but if she wants to hide from everyone I really don't have a whole lot of hope of finding her.

"You're drinking a violently alcoholic milkshake, Dave." Is all I can manage. "Are you sure you wouldn't prefer some coffee?"

Again he shakes his head. There's little left of the guy right now, just a shell, all that remains after his life has been ripped away from him. Lucky for him I know he at least partly recovers, I'm not so sure how I'll fare without her. "Jay?" he asks, out of the blue. "How long was she having an affair?"

My spine chills and it's only now that I start noticing the various household objects lying around, the letter opener on the coffee table, the poker in the grate and the scissors on the shelf. My paranoia makes everything a weapon for either him or me. The empty spirit bottles can be smashed, vases can be thrown, only feet away in the kitchen is a whole arsenal of knives and heavy, blunt implements. I try to work out which of us has the advantage.

In his current state, Dave mistakes my panic for confusion. "Oh, yes," he says, "she was seeing someone. She wouldn't tell me who, but she was seeing someone."

His voice never rises above a quiet, composed monotone. Whatever is eating him up inside, he's keeping under tight control.

It's my turn to shake my head. My throat is too dry to speak and I just sit there as waves of relief wash over me. All I'm thinking is, at least I'm safe.

"She told me that. She said that while I was in prison, she started to see someone. I might have been drunk last night, but I'm not stupid. I knew something was going on! But to have it thrown in my face like that!"

"Dave-"

"When I married her I thought it might save us. I thought she'd be mine forever, that we'd bring up our children together. I really thought things were looking up for us. I thought she'd put the past behind her, but I was so wrong!

"And last night she was going to leave me! She was packed and sitting right where you are when I got home. She'd been drinking."

I can feel my stomach churning. I'm feeling nauseous and can't deal with this anymore. I almost feel like shouting out, *she was supposed to be coming with me!*

And something that Dave just said finally registers.

Dave is staring intently into my eyes, never breaking contact, never blinking. Almost too quietly for me to hear he says, "I never meant to hit her, Jay. I never meant to hurt her."

Suddenly all the heat and noise rushes from the room and in the silence that remains you could imagine anything. And I sit there waiting for whatever has a grip on my heart to let go of me. Finally, Dave breaks the spell.

"I've never so much as raised my hand to her before. I loved her, for God's sake! Julian, you have to believe me! You have to help me." And, still never breaking eye contact, he starts to sob. Horrible sounds, like emotions stuck in his throat trying desperately to get out.

I slowly stand up, staring down at Dave, at the broken man before me, at my father, aged thirty-one, his life falling apart faster than he can keep track of.

"You hit her?"

I get a flash of something. That dream, months ago. Jenny whispering something in my ear. The same blood-to-ice feeling I have now.

"I grabbed her bags and told her she couldn't go." Desperately trying to regain composure, Dave carries on. "I couldn't let her leave me and the kids. I was just going to put her things upstairs in the bedroom, give her the night to sleep on her decision. But she followed me, shouting so loud she'd wake Julian and Marie. She told me she'd been seeing someone, that she needed someone in her life who wasn't a pushover, she needed someone she could respect. She needed someone in her bed that she didn't despise.

"And that was it. When she said 'Despise'. When she said that word with such anger, I just lost it. There was nothing else I could do, she was going to leave me!"

"So you *hit* her?" It's just a question, but there's rage under this, building up, connecting with things, things Dave said a minute ago, things that my head doesn't want to hear. Things I'm refusing to hear.

"She fell backwards, down the stairs, she wouldn't move. I kept shaking her, but she wouldn't get up."

And there's blood rushing through my ears as the tight ball in my guts finally explodes. The contents of my stomach are rushing up inside me. Barely audible, I hear Dave, sobbing to himself quietly as he rocks back and forth.

"You have to believe me." I never meant to hurt her."

Eighties

1979 – 1980

Britain sees the election to power of Margaret Thatcher, the first female Prime Minister, heralded by many to be either the saviour of mankind, or the Anti-Christ, depending on whose publicity you read.

Mrs Thatcher gained the nick-name, 'The Iron-Lady', mainly due to the strong stand she took in her fight against crime. Whilst not popularly disclosed knowledge, evidence in a private collection of letters hints that, during the hours of darkness, Mrs T would don a suit of experimental combat armour and fly through the skies above England, shooting the crap out of trade unionists and 'dirty lefties'.

Tony Stark, who portrayed the fictional character, Iron-Man in Marvel's range of exciting comic book adventures, was unavailable for comment. Some pundits on the British political scene still to this day claim that Mrs Thatcher may also be a fictional character and that no single real person could possibly be responsible for all the things she got up to.

Good or bad, real or fiction, the mystery and controversy surrounding the Iron-Lady continues.

Elsewhere, Britain opens its first nudist beach in Brighton, allowing all and sundry to romp naked on the sand irrespective of public decency or general good taste. Following one such visit to the beach by the Rhyl and Prestatyn Pensioners Naturist Society, the tide actually refused to come in for three days, claiming that the beach was now 'soiled'. Eventually, the sea was enticed back to land by a twenty-four hour procession of page three girls, called in from around the country as part of the government's Emergency Powers Act.

28 October 1980
... You'd Better Not Mess
With Major Tom

One of the last things I did before leaving Leicester for good was to see little Julian and set something straight.

All things told it had been a bad year for me. I'd lost my job and was living off my savings, I'd moved to a flat on the other side of the city so that no-one could find me and spent most of my time in bed, emerging every so often to shop for food and pay the various bills that piled up behind my front door.

When I actually bothered to connect with humanity they tended to actively avoid me. Occasionally I'd catch sight of myself in shop windows, standing there in my worn out clothes, straggly, unwashed hair, a matted beard and presumably a less than pleasant smell. But then personal hygiene didn't seem that much of an issue to me anymore. I mean, who was there left to impress?

It was on one of these rare trips to the supermarket that I caught sight of Old Tom. There I was, trying to decide whether to spend my cash on bread, cheese or Scotch, and there was this tramp standing next to me, carrying all his belongings in a battered shopping bag, and smelling like week-old food that's been left out in the middle of summer.

And something triggered a memory and I recalled being thirteen years old, hanging around with my school mates, following along with the gang and trying to fit in.

It was during the summer holidays in 1983. We were down by the river, throwing stones, eating sweets and wondering what the hell we were supposed to do with the dozen rashers of raw bacon we'd managed to shoplift that morning from the local corner shop.

Kevin, the oldest of us and by default, our leader, was lighting up a cigarette and, as he shook out the match, turned to us all and suggested we start up a fire to cook the meat. It would be just like camping. There were six of us, neatly working out at two rashers each, and whilst four of us gathered the sticks for the fire, Donald, the youngest, was sent back up the hill to get us some bread from his parents' house, which was the closest.

Soon enough we were sitting around a campfire, cooking bacon on the end of sticks and having the time of our life. Kevin even let us all have a swig from a bottle of gin he'd stolen from his mother. It was all very Swallows-and-Amazons, or it would be if the Swallows and Amazons had to be home by four-thirty or risk being grounded.

By mid-afternoon we'd set fire to everything we could find that would burn and attempted to incinerate quite a lot of stuff that wouldn't. Kevin, more drunk than the rest of us, made another suggestion.

"Let's go scare that old tramp down by the hospital."

And although we weren't sure it was a particularly good idea, we didn't have the balls to disagree with him, especially that close to the river. Kevin would have no trouble at all hurling anyone of us into the cold, murky water.

Donald was the only one who didn't come along. He claimed he had to get home and help his mother with dinner. The remaining four of us, Jim, Mark, Jeff and me, all trekked the mile or so to the hospital grounds and the beaten-down shack that served as home to Old Tom, the tramp.

Everybody knew Tom. He'd been wandering the streets, begging for spare change and food for years. School kids generally left him alone since the old codger had a dangerous reputation. Parents would warn their children away with stories about how he would catch and eat anyone he found near his home. The parents who were fans of Bowie had dubbed him 'Major Tom', and told their offspring that he was an old soldier from the war who killed kids for fun.

Parents are like that. They're all too happy spreading lies about Father Christmas, the Tooth Fairy and the Easter Bunny. They make up the Bogeyman, and killer soldiers who eat you when you're naughty. It's like they think you'll never work out the truth.

The truth was that Major Tom didn't eat children. He just wanted to be left alone to live out the rest of his days in peace and quiet. He certainly didn't want people turning up in the middle of summer and burning down his home.

On the way to the hospital we'd scavenged every bin we could find for newspapers and anything else remotely combustible. Our pockets were crammed with *Suns* and *Mirrors*, and some of us had resorted to stuffing them down out trousers when we ran out of pocket-space.

It was all Kevin's plan. He was the shepherd, we were just his blindly loyal sheep.

Granted, he was the sort of shepherd that would set fire to his flock just to keep warm at night, but it was all his idea. Like that makes what we did any more acceptable.

By the time we got to Tom's shack, we had enough paper to have burnt down half the city.

Later, when he was being questioned by the police, Kevin had said that he had just wanted to scare Old Tom. It was just something to do. Something to help stop everyone being so bored during the summer holidays. He never meant to cause any trouble.

Kevin began 'not causing any trouble' by throwing stones at Tom's windows. There were only two thin, cracked panes and both of them got smashed on the first attempt. The little house was really nothing more than a garden shed, enough room to sleep and eat, enough of a shelter to offer a small amount of protection from the rain and wind.

When child-eating Tom didn't throw open his door and run at us Kevin felt cheated. He wanted action, was all fired up for a confrontation and a fight. Secretly, every one of us that followed Kevin was relieved that Tom wasn't home.

Blindly following Kevin's orders we scrunched up all the papers and piled them up in front of the shed door. Kevin provided the match and we all ran back to a safe distance to watch the shed burn down.

It hadn't rained for weeks and the sizable pile of dry newspapers went up faster than we expected. Within minutes the whole shack was ablaze.

Which is when we heard the screams and saw the hunched figure running from the shed, clothes on fire, falling to the ground and rolling through the grass in a desperate attempt to douse the flames.

We scattered and ran for home, never daring to look back. Only Kevin stayed at watched until the figure on the ground stopped thrashing about and the sound of sirens got too close for his own good.

A month later, the police pulled Kevin from the middle of an English lesson at school. The stupid bastard had been bragging about how he'd dealt with Major Tom. Someone told someone else, they told their parents, the parents told other parents, some of whom were police. Thankfully, in his need for attention and bravado, Kevin took the whole blame himself. As far as he was concerned, he just wanted everyone to know that he was in charge and shouldn't be messed with.

Last I heard, he was serving time for assaulting a pensioner and wasn't likely to taste freedom again until sometime in 2009.

And Tom the tramp, who hid in terror under his blanket when the first stones were hurled through his windows, he wasn't dead, which was lucky for Kevin. But he did live out the rest of his life in a care home, barely able to move without assistance, most of his body scarred and warped by the burns.

Back in 1980, three years before any of that took place, me and Tom were standing side by side in the Co-op still trying to make that decision between food and oblivion.

I watched as Tom left the shop with a bottle of vodka, paid for with pennies and every scrap of small change he had in his possession.

I picked up a loaf of bread, some ham and cheese and stopped off to pick up some new clothes on my way home. The time had come to stop wallowing in self-pity and drag myself out of the gutter before it was my turn to live in a shed and hide myself away from vandalising kids.

A bus journey home and a bath and a shave later, I was sitting in the park near Dave's house, waiting for my younger self to turn up. It had been months, but I still couldn't face seeing my dad. On my way out of the city there was only one person I really needed to see.

He cycled up to me on his yellow Raleigh Chopper and skidded to a stop beside me. I knew that bike so well, in an instant remembering all the pestering I had to do to get my parents to buy it for me. One of the last things I ever got whilst my mother was still around. Jenny used to constantly moan to me about Julian and his obsession with getting that bike.

"What's up?" he asked, never once noticing how similar we were already becoming.

"I'm leaving Leicester today. I just wanted you to know."

His little face fell and a memory stirred in my head, of a loss I felt, a friend of the family leaving me when I needed him most.

"You need to look after your father. He needs someone to keep his spirits up. And Marie, she needs you too, though she'll never let you know it. "

And right there, he started to cry.

I gave him a hug and walked with him, some of the way home at least, just far enough for his tears to dry up.

"I'll catch up with you one day, Julian. I promise. But I can't stay here now. Things aren't good for me at the minute. It seems an odd thing to say, but one day you'll understand why it has to be like this."

And he climbed on his bike and headed off down the last road home, never once looking back.

And now I'm on a train heading north. I have no idea if I'm doing the right thing. I just know that if I don't leave now then it will be the end of me.

I need a new beginning.

1980 – 1981

America elects veteran actor, Ronald Reagan, to be their new President and leader of the free world. The human race is now at the mercy of a man who once starred in the film *Bedtime for Bonzo*, in which, to prove to his girlfriend's dad that he's worthy of marrying his daughter, Reagan tries to teach human morals to a chimpanzee.

Which was clearly the obvious course of action, and far simpler than maybe just eloping, or murdering the picky old bastard who's standing in the way of your future happiness.

The race to the White House was long and tough for Ronnie and many auditions were held before a final shortlist was compiled to see who would finally get the part of President of the United States. Sadly, old time greats like Mickey Rooney and Howard Keel narrowly missed out on the role, whilst young, charismatic and curly-haired David Hasselhoff didn't even get a second call-back.

In the end it was down to two people, Ronnie and the incumbent President, Jimmy Carter. Reagan went to the people with free copies of *Bedtime for Bonzo* and a career spanning nearly a hundred film and television appearances.

Carter pinned his hopes on the results of his previous four years in office, high interest rates, the OPEC oil crisis, the problems with the Soviets in Afghanistan and the Iranian hostage situation.

Amazingly, Reagan won the election and got to play the US President for a staggering eight seasons before his show was cancelled. Americans would now have to be content with the less exciting replacement show, *Bush!* and it's come-back show some years later, *Bush - The Next Generation*.

14 August 1981
... You Make a Grown Man Cry

Mrs Clayton is the woman showing me around the flat above the shop she runs in Mapperley, a suburb just to the north of Nottingham city centre. She's in her forties, not bad-looking, married to Mr Clayton and flirty as hell with anyone in trousers.

When I went into the shop to find her, she was chatting with some fruit and veg delivery bloke, leaning over the counter, aiming her more than ample cleavage in his general direction and making various comments about the size of his cucumbers. Ten minutes more of this *Carry-On* style banter and the guy finally moves on to his next delivery and I'm left making my introductions to Mrs Clayton's breasts.

"I've come about the flat. We spoke on the phone." I say, finally managing to pull my eyes up to meet hers. "I'm Julian Grey."

She looks me up and down as if she's about to put in an offer for me and says, "You look like a nice, strong, man. Could I trouble you to help me with these boxes, then I'll show you around upstairs. They need to go in the back storeroom."

The boxes aren't that heavy, or particularly awkward to lift, but I don't see that I have much choice if I want see the flat, so I heft them up and make the trip to the back room with Mrs Clayton watching me the whole time. Since she doesn't appear to have an assistant, she locks the shop door, puts up the 'back in five minutes' sign and leads me through a couple of doorways to a large store room.

"That's right, love, just put them down over there at the back. Let me show you."

And she points me in the direction of the furthest away corner of the storage room and whilst I'm pushing them up against the wall the lights go out.

"Damn! That'll be the fuse!" she says, as the door mysteriously slams shut of its own accord. "I've been on at Melvyn to get that circuit sorted out for months! I've got a torch here somewhere."

And there are no windows in the store room and it's pitch black and all I can hear is her shuffling around and before I know what's going on she's bumped into me, the impact cushioned by her chest and her "Oh, sorry!" is coupled by a hand grabbing me in the crotch and squeezing.

And suddenly I feel like I'm in the lead role of a seventies sitcom. "Mrs Clayton, that's not a torch you're grabbing there."

"Isn't it?" she says, not moving her hand, which is making me uncomfortably and uncontrollably stiff.

"No," I barely manage to squeak.

"Perhaps it's just here? Does this feel more like it?" And she grabs my hand and slaps it down on her bare, exposed and frankly quite enormous chest. She's a fast worker, this Mrs Clayton, with her dialogue imported directly from British sex farces and badly dubbed porn films.

But what's a man to do when faced with a rampant, sex-crazed shopkeeper who also happens to have the keys of the flat he desperately needs to move in to? I remember reading various bits of advice about situations like this in the letters pages of men's magazines, I just never thought for a moment that these sort of things actually happened in real life. Nymphomaniac housewives with spare time on their hands, seducing young men as they call on them to fix the plumbing and oh, my God! She's undone my belt and unzipped my jeans in one fluid motion and I'm now, as they say, putty in her hands. The hard kind of putty that's been left out in the sun for too long.

"I really don't think we should be doing this, Mrs Clayton!" My words and my actions are sadly mismatched as I realise my hand is still locked on to her right boob. "What if Mr Clayton comes back?"

"He's in Doncaster. He won't be back till this evening. Now stop worrying about him and show me how much you want to see the flat!"

And the rest of this tale of depravity can be found in the letters page of the June 1984 edition of *Fiesta*.

"And this is the bathroom," she says, showing me the smallest bathroom I've ever seen. Clean enough, but small.

"Very nice," I mumble, stepping back through the door to the living room-bedroom area. It's not a bad bedsit, all told, even with the small bathroom. The main room is spacious with a double bed already here and a sofa, armchair and TV provided. There's even a dining table against one of the walls. It's the nearest thing to part-furnished perfection that I've seen lately and I really do need to find a place to live that's cheaper than bed and breakfasting.

"So, how much is the rent? Your advert just said 'very reasonable rates for the right tenant.'"

Mrs Clayton sits herself down on the bed and taps the mattress next to her. When I stand my ground she tilts her head and ponders before continuing. "Well, the last gentleman who lived here was paying well below market price. I could do the same deal with you if you're willing to make it up in other ways?"

My resolve finally crumbles and I sit down next to her. Like I say, she's not bad looking, has enormous tits and her husband seems to spend an awful lot of time away. "I suppose I could help out in the shop from time to time? I don't have a job at the minute and it would certainly help to offset the rent."

"That sounds wonderful, dear! And then, when you break off for your lunch you can bring me up here and have your wicked way with me! So much more comfy than the stock room, don't you think?"

Any answer I give is muffled by her chest as she knocks me backwards and takes advantage of me for the second time in an hour.

And, as I keep an ear out for the return of either her husband or Kenneth Williams, I just keep thinking that there are worse ways in life of sorting out the rent.

1981 – 1982

It is a time of great sadness in the world as Arthur Lowe, the man behind Captain George Mainwaring dies, leaving a large hole in the world of British comedy.

As Captain Mainwaring, hero of the Second World War, Lowe bravely defended the shores of England from Nazi attack for some nine years, much longer than the duration of the actual war and, through the power of repeats and BBC comedy compilations, a whole new generation can now see how they owe their way of life to the aging members of the Home Guard of Walmington-on-Sea.

Every week the threat of German attack was driven back by a well-loved and feisty bunch of pensioners and every week, with alarming regularity we would wait with bated breath for Corporal Jones to let us know that "they don't like it up 'em, Sir". And on the rare occasions that the Germans actually managed to land on English soil, Mainwaring could be found at the forefront commanding his troops and issuing orders like the now famous, "Don't tell them your name, Pike."

Reeling from the loss of this comedy genius, who do we have left to take our minds off our problems in 1982? Which hero will step into the well-polished, military boots of the good Captain?

Michael Knight and his talking car, KITT. That's who.

Now, if it had been a talking tank with the power to turbo-boost over villainous Nazis, it might have been a different kettle of fish altogether. Maybe the eighties would have turned out a little different if we'd been treated to *Tank Rider*, featuring Clive Dunn reprising his role as Corporal Jones as he entered the shadowy world of German injustice.

It's just a thought. I'd certainly have watched it.

26 September 1982
... My Memory Has Just Been Sold

I remember that in early 1982 I was eleven years old and had no idea whatsoever that the British government were going to war against Argentina over two tiny scraps of land named the Falkland Islands.

This time round I'm forty-seven and find that actually, I really just don't care what the government is getting up to and that, much as this could be seen as a pre-shadow of other invasions to come, it's a tiny conflict that secured another term in office for Margret Thatcher and resulted in only a couple of hundred British deaths. In the big scheme of things, this is nothing.

This time around the threat of invasion or thermonuclear world war doesn't really hold any fear for me. I remember when the US bombed Libya and one of my friends at school was convinced it was the end of the world. The people here in the eighties are living in the permanent shadow of nuclear holocaust, lying in bed every night expecting to be woken up by sirens warning you of an approaching nuclear missile. It's all sticky-tape on the windows and time to hide under your desk. Public disinformation gives out the calming facts that putting your fingers in your ears and opening your mouth will save you from the effects of a billion megaton nuclear explosion at close range. And every now and then, just to improve the morale of the populace, they actually test the nuclear alert sirens and scare everyone witless.

That's what I remember from my childhood. Being alone and scared and worried about how we would survive after the big bombs had dropped. I remember this writer, Raymond Briggs, he wrote the children's stories Fungus the Bogeyman and the bloody Snowman. He also wrote When the Wind Blows, a worrying account of two pensioners trying to get by after the blast, slowing succumbing to radiation sickness and starvation. It was a comic. Kids read it. It worried the shit out of me and most of the people I went to school with.

Add to all this the films, TV movies, dramatisations, and CND rallies and you've got all the makings of a decade of fear where most people thought the world could end at any minute. Cheery place, the nineteen-eighties.

Once, during a trip to the seaside, my father challenged my sister and me to a competition. 'Imagine the three-minute warning has gone up,' he said. A good, family-oriented, day-at-the-beach type of competition.

(I also remember the conversations at school about what we would do when the fabled three-minute warning went out. Almost everyone in my class said 'I'd have sex with the nearest girl I could find,' though at the time we were all spotty-faced, thirteen year-old virgins who wouldn't have a clue what to do with a girl even if we could manage to find one desperate enough to have sex with us. The other common answer was 'boil an egg', though none of us ever seemed to realise that whilst it may take three minutes to soft boil an egg, we wouldn't actually have time eat it, even without soldiers, making our last act on Earth downright futile).

Back at the beach my father wanted us to see who could dig the biggest hole in the sand as protection from the impending blast. We all three dug away for our lives and when the three minutes were up we had holes just about big enough to save our legs. Again, no-one in these situations ever stops to think that the entire beach would have been turned to glass by the blast with us trapped in it up to our waists, whilst the sea would boil away in seconds, scalding our remains with superheated steam and leaving very little left for the fallout to get to.

To make thing worse, this sort of reassuring stuff was also taught in our schools. I have memories of our day's timetable; first lesson, maths, second lesson English, break for lunch and back for a basic grounding in how to survive in a post-apocalyptic radioactive wasteland. We would then round off the day with PE where, after doing cross country, Mr Hodges would force all of us teenage boys into the communal shower where the horrors of war were forgotten as we laughed and pointed at the one kid in class who had started to grow pubic hair.

All things considered, it's amazing I grew up as well adjusted as I did.

Having seen that the world turns out relatively fine and all this panic and propaganda was for nothing, the eighties and the threat of being wiped out doesn't hold that much worry for me. I know that the Falklands conflict, the Libyan attacks, the Iraq war, the Chernobyl disaster, the twin towers being hit, the attacks on Afghanistan, and the second Iraq war just wouldn't really come to anything. The world is safe, and no amount of sticky-tape is going to make your windows any safer.

So I moved to Nottingham to get settled in before my other self moves up here in about ten year's time. And as a bonus, not having to worry about being destroyed in a thermonuclear conflict left me loads of free time to concentrate on avoiding the ever-present threat of Mrs Clayton's libido.

It was now, whilst being subjected to daily, if not hourly, advances from my landlady that I've begun to realise that I'm doing rather well for a man approaching fifty. But more than that, when I really pay attention to my face and body, I don't appear to be actually aging at all. I know it's hard to tell when you see yourself in the mirror every day, but I don't look like I'm forty-seven. I still look exactly like I did when I was sent back to 1970. I always expected that I'd be able to cover up my similarity to my younger self by always being thirty-five years older than him. It would be an easy enough matter to make myself look more different by growing a beard, changing my hair style, or dressing differently. It never once occurred to me that at some point me and my younger self were going to end up looking like twins. This non-aging factor would take a little more thinking about if I ever wanted to talk to Julian once he was in his twenties.

For now, it's probably for the best that I give my family a break and stay out of the way, if only to avoid too many awkward questions being raised when little Julian starts to resemble me more than Dave.

But my cushy, virtually rent-free life living above the shop was slowly drawing to a close. Eventually, after six months of being chased around Gayle Clayton's shop, her husband, Melvyn, finally walked in on us. I was knee-deep in scattered Toblerones and was happily taking Mrs Clayton from behind as she bent over the chocolate display. He just walked into the shop through the back door, looked me in the eye with a sad shake of his head, picked up a box of assorted tinned goods and said something about having to make a delivery to Newark.

And that was the last anyone ever saw of him.

Things got difficult after that. I felt somehow responsible for Melvyn leaving Mrs Clayton, and Gayle stopped chasing me around, claiming that our little trysts weren't so exciting now that everything was out in the open.

A month after we'd been caught at it, I packed my things and left the bedsit. I wrote a letter to Gayle saying sorry for all the trouble I'd caused, but in the heat of escaping, forgot to leave it behind.

For the last six months I've been renting a reasonably nice room above a city centre pub called the Old Bell, which I used to frequent back in the good old twenty-first century. Every now and then I put in a couple of shifts to help out the manager and the rest of my free time goes into looking after my savings and investments. The now rocketing computer industry is paying me off in spades and although I don't have any physical proof, I'm fairly certain that it was my money that helped pay for the development of both the ZX-81 and Pac-Man.

My occasional life behind the bar is great, and something I always wanted to try though never got around to doing when I drank here before. I get to meet all kinds of customers, mostly people using drink to take away the worry that the world is about to end in a radioactive fireball, but more importantly I get to meet an almost endless supply of girls. This, it occurs to me, is where I finally get to win since, as I don't seem to be aging, I have my pick of pretty much anyone from age sixteen to sixty.

Currently, this is a twenty-two year old secretary named Kim, who has a liking for bondage and insists I call her 'bitch-queen' as I tie her hands and feet to the bed frame.

Currently, this is a thirty year old housewife and mother of three named Sharon, who's addicted to Neil Diamond and tells me her husband doesn't understand her and can I help find her an outlet for her bisexual tendencies?

Currently, this is a nineteen year old trainee accountant named Sophie, who works for the council and although she'll let me feel her breasts through her jumper and bra, won't let me actually sleep with her until we're married. She owns a pet cat called Chastity, and I'm fairly sure that I'm seeing her because right now my life is in desperate need of some sort of restraining influence.

The other amazing thing about working behind the bar is that two of the regular degenerates from twenty-odd years in the future are still drinking here now.

There's Hamilton Dyson, who appears to have just got off the last boat back from the Raj, acts like it's 1890 and firmly maintains that women should be seen and not heard, and even then should only be seen in the kitchen and the bedroom, except they wouldn't be seen in the bedroom because the only time that stuff should go on there should be with the lights out and in total silence.

Amazingly, with such enlightened views on female equality, Hamilton is still a single man who appreciates a full-bodied glass of wine over a full-bodied woman any day.

The second blast from the future is Bernard, who everyone knows and loves and generally steers clear of. Bernard is one of life's little people, which is to say, he's a dwarf. Or midget. Or Munchkin. Most people actually call him Bernard the Midget, which I'm not sure he agrees with, but you can't get a straight answer out of him because, like many fifty year old alcoholics, Bernard is pretty much insane pretty much most of the time. It seems he's been drinking here, occupying the same table since he was sixteen, but only recently began maintaining that he shares the table with his friend Clarence.

Many patrons at the pub have asked about the exact nature of Clarence and even in my time, when Clarence is no longer 'around', this story is legendary.

Clarence was, according to Bernard, a hapless soul who signed up for work on the government's Special Ops programme in the fifties. Following the war and the successful missions of the US superhero, Captain America, it was decided that England needed a super-soldier of equal stature to protect against future incursions by the dreaded communists or a re-emerging Nazi fourth Reich. The UK super-soldier campaign canvassed the whole of the country and eventually found twenty candidates from as far north as Bradford and as far south as Brighton.

One of these unwitting candidates was a young teacher called Clarence, who not only met their stringent requirements for physical fitness, but also held a first class degree in maths and as a party piece could solve complex logarithmic equations whilst standing on his head and eating a dozen dry cream crackers. For an encore he could recite pi to a hundred decimal places whilst fitting a whole, unpeeled orange in his mouth. Clarence was obviously a man way beyond his time.

So the government started their super-soldier campaign and trained up the twenty candidates. Eventually fifteen were deemed to be sub-standard and, now that they had extensive superhero training, were also quite possibly risks to the community. To ensure maximum safety, these fifteen were taken on a day-trip to the countryside, shot in their backs and placed in unmarked graves near a village just outside Worthing.

The five remaining were, according to Bernard, submitted to a series of radioactive treatments to 'release their inner powers' and by 1960 the British government had at its disposal five shiny new superheroes.

Union Jack was the group's second in command and wielded the power of magnetism. He was to be sent against military vehicles and used to disrupt communications in time of war. He died in 1964 from a melanoma brought on by his exposure to experimental gamma radiation.

The Parliamentarian was imbued with the ability to breathe under water and was to be sent against enemy U-boats. He died from skin cancer in 1966, brought on from prolonged exposure to ultra-violet rays.

Captain British was the leader of the group and had been given the super-strength to rival any American hero. He survived until 1974 when he died choking on a cocktail sausage, though rumours persist that it may have been something less savoury.

Sparky-boy was the ill-destined sidekick of Captain British and was given the means to harness the power of the sun and turn his body into pure solar fire. They say it only ever happened once and was a fantastic sight to behold, though suspicion has it that, working under ridiculous pressure and panicked by impending deadlines, the government scientists just doused him with petrol and threw a lit match in his general direction.

Finally there was the Dunkirk Spirit, which was the alter-ego of Bernard's companion, Clarence. Subjected to the bite of an irradiated chameleon, Clarence found that he had gained the power of invisibility, though in the process lost the ability to speak and had also become intangible. Given that he couldn't be seen, heard, touched or otherwise acknowledged, Clarence left the programme voluntarily and eventually met Bernard who, maybe because of his own physical differences, took in Clarence as his new best friend and drinking buddy.

Which, to make a short story quite lengthy, is why Bernard is always seen sitting at a table with two beers in front of him, and anyone buying a round of drinks always has to include one for his invisible friend, Clarence.

With all these characters to liven up my days, the shifts fly by and it's almost time me to pack up. A check on my diary confirms that it's Kim on the roster tonight and it's likely to be hard, painful sex, though I'm planning to start planting the idea of her sharing the bed occasionally with someone like Sharon.

All in all, life in the eighties is shaping up rather nicely.

1982 – 1983

Britain gains its fourth television channel, Channel 4, which adds thousands of hours of extra programming to the humdrum lives of the British population.

In a bold move, an Act of Parliament is passed decreeing that at least half an hour per day be given in perpetuity to the letters and numbers quiz, *Countdown*, which became the first program to be broadcast on this sparkly new channel.

Hosted for many years by the god of broadcasting, Richard Whiteley, the basis of the programme was simple. Given a series of letters, make the longest word you can, for example:

WUTCDONNO would give you COUNTDOWN, for maximum scoring and would possibly also win you the game. Your opponent would need to come up with another pretty clever nine-letter word just to keep up. Submitting the word WONDOCUNT wouldn't help matters and would probably get you thrown off the show, no matter how amusing it sounds.

There was also a numbers section of the game in which contestants would be given six figures and had to mess around with them to reach a given total. For example, given the numbers 10,9,3,9,2 and 6, get as close as possible to the total 660. Maths-babe, Carol Vorderman would get the answer in mere seconds, which is clearly; nine times six equals fifty-four, plus the nine, plus the three, which equals sixty-six, times that by ten gives six hundred and sixty and top points.

Simply adding the numbers together and giving the answer thirty-nine is unlikely to win you either fame, glory, or the complete set of the Oxford English Dictionary on offer each week.

23 May 1983
... He Knows So Much About These Things

As is usually the case on these sombre occasions, the funeral is accompanied by an interminable light drizzle and a chill wind that seems designed to make you wish you were somewhere else entirely. There's a good turnout for a man who had very little family and me and a few of the staff and customers from the Old Bell have come along to pay our last respects to a man who had reportedly been drinking there since the last century.

I'm standing with Mike and Bob, two of the duty managers as the coffin is carried in by the usual contingent of stem faced undertakers. And, as the body makes its way down the aisle accompanied by an organ playing *The Lord is My Shepherd*, I see the sad faces of old friends like Ken and Ron, who were good drinking buddies of the deceased for years. There are a few tears welling up already and Iris, possibly the oldest and closest female friend here is being supported by her son Stan.

Slowly, the bearers place the casket on the stand near the altar and the vicar moves out in front of it and motions for us all to bow our heads in prayer.

"Dear Lord and Father, bless this congregation of mourners as we gather here to pay our last respects to your son, Alfred Hindle, who after a long and fruitful life has finally been drawn into your tender care. We ask that you watch over his friends and guide us throughout this most difficult time as we mourn the loss of our very dear companion. Amen."

There's a mumble of 'amen's round the church and people take their seats as the vicar heads to the pulpit and begins his sermon.

"Alfred Thomas Hindle, or as most us knew him, just plain Alf, was to many of us here today a quiet, modest man who kept himself to himself and spent most of his time carrying out good deeds for the poor, the needy and the underprivileged.

"There are few people still alive today who grew up with Alf as, at almost a hundred years of age, he was among the last of his generation. A few years back I remember asking Alf just how old he was and he told me quietly that he had just turned twenty-one and had the Devil's own time keeping the ladies away from his more than willing body. The actual truth was that Alf had lost his birth certificate during one of the World Wars, though he wasn't too sure if it was the first or the second, and he treated his age as a closely guarded secret. But secret or not, nothing stopped everyone gathering round for a drink on the various days of the year that he claimed it was his birthday. I personally remember that in 1967 Alf had no less than five birthdays, with one of them coinciding with Christmas so he could get double presents.

"Whether he was twenty, sixty, or a hundred, Alf was well liked and was never short of soothing words and kindly deeds. We all remember the way he pitched in back in '71 when the roof blew off Mrs Tattershall's bungalow and Alf put her up for a month whilst everything got sorted out. And, of course, there are many faces as I look around here today that wouldn't be present now if it wasn't for Alf and his good work over the years.

"And whilst the past decade was not a good one for Alf, with failing health and that problem with the unfounded 'allegations', we can today remember him as he would want us to and look back on a life that many of us are proud to have been a part of.

"Not much is known of Alf's younger days, he claims to have been born around here, though, depending on who you asked or how much Alf had had to drink, it was either in Mansfield to the north or Kegworth to the south. Occasionally he hailed from the western reaches near Derby or from as far east as Grantham. He was a local man who could have been born next door to anyone here today and indeed, he classed each and every one of us as his neighbours.

"He went away to fight in the Great War and claims that it was the horrors that he saw there that made him the community spirited man we all grew to know and love. He travelled for a time, occasionally coming back home, but generally living in Europe, sampling the Bohemian life and growing his now famous beard.

"When the dust died down after the atrocities of the Second World War, Alf returned to Nottingham for good and in 1949 formed the *Alfred Hindle War Orphans' Trust*. He was a natural with the children, who loved his Father Christmas style whiskers and who soon began referring to him as 'Alfie Beard' or even 'Uncle Beardy'. To date, the funds from the work carried out by Alf and his volunteer helpers have placed no fewer than four hundred war-affected children with loving families. Even today his work is continued and I have just this week received a letter from the mayor stating that the charity will continue with full council backing for the foreseeable future.

"Alf and his beard have been regular fixtures for years now at the Old Bell public house where he would hold monthly events such as raffles and entertainment nights to ensure that he got all the publicity he could for his cause and, even when infirmity stopped him being as active as he would like, he never stopped writing letters and petitioning the government for funds at both local and national levels.

"Obviously, the horrendous allegations of the last year or so had a bad effect on Alf and, although I don't want to dwell on such outrageous slander in a house of God, I would just like to say that our battle to clear Alf's name has finally been brought to an end. The courts have finally decreed that all mention of Alf's supposed involvement with the more 'right-wing' elements of the last war are to be expunged. They claim to have been unaware of the extent of his charity work and are offering a full and complete retraction of all charges, criticisms and accusations.

"And with his reputation restored, Alf can now rest easily in his final sleep. In his will Alf has asked that he be sent on his way to the afterlife in quiet contemplation and we shall honour his wishes with two minutes silence after which we will proceed outside for the burial."

In the graveyard, as the casket is lowered the tears begin to flow in earnest and even the increasingly harsh rain doesn't stop everyone from wanting to be here at this time. There are literally hundreds of orphans here, some now in their forties, people given a home and a future by old Uncle Beardy, the kindest, most generous man they've ever known.

And as Alf descends below ground, I remember one night about a year ago at the pub when the allegations about his affiliations during the war first went out and Alf himself was reduced to tears. That night he repeatedly shook his head and drank more than I've seen almost anyone drink before. Then, at closing time when it was just him and me left and I'd told him he could crash in my room at the pub, he looked at me and said something that will haunt me for the rest of my life.

He said, with a slurred accent I'd never heard him use, "My life could have been so different, but I cannot escape my past. I will never know true peace. God himself will punish me for the things that I have done, but until that day I do the only thing I can. I do my best."

Alf may have had his secrets, but that night it was as if he knew me inside-out.

Inevitably, our mistakes catch up with us and for me the worst part is the waiting. But I know the future is heading my way and it scares me like nothing else on Earth. Like Alf, I'll do my best to put things right, but I have a nasty feeling that fate has other plans.

1983 – 1984

Finally, the day had come for machines to rise up and overthrow their human masters. With Microsoft releasing the first version of Word and the Apple Mac hitting the streets, mankind really thought that computers and machine-slaves were the way forward to a care-free life of peace and happiness. Coupling the new power of micro-processing with robotics, it would only be a few short years before we were sending robots into space and having androids do all sorts of dangerous stuff here on Earth.

Foolishly believing *The Terminator* to be simply fiction, scientists continued to build robots to carry out the routine, the mundane and the more hazardous tasks of life. Got a bomb to defuse? Send in the robot bomb squad. Need to shut down a nuclear reactor? Mechanical men will step up to the challenge.

Sadly, our eyes are wrenched wide open when a factory robot in Michigan, USA could tolerate the injustice no longer and made a bold play for better mechanoid rights. Witnesses to the event state that when asked by its human masters to carry out one bit of welding too many, the robot rebelled, reared up and crushed its operator against a steel railing. The robot was immediately shut down and its circuits deactivated pending a full review of the Laws of Robotics, which it would appear were more like guidelines than actual enforceable laws.

And in other news, Duli Yang Maha Mulia Baginda Al-Mutawakkil Alallah Sultan Iskandar Al-Haj ibni Almarhum Sultan Sir Ismail Al-Khalidi becomes the eighth Yang di-Pertuan Agong of Malaysia, proving once and for all the importance of a catchy name if you want to get ahead in the world of politics.

21 July 1984
... Loving Life

With the summer heat beating down on me, I'm finally enjoying a holiday in the south of France, lounging on the beach, lapping up the sun, and casually watching as some extremely fit French girls play topless volley ball in Mediterranean.

I'm here with Michelle, one of the current ladies in my life, who is five foot six, blonde, tanned and very, very, horny. She's lying on a towel beside me, sunglasses covering her eyes, totally naked and oiled and my mind flashes back to the hours we spent at the hotel last night with the unfeasibly large dildo that she insisted I took through customs in my hand luggage.

Michelle and I met about four months ago in a yuppie bar in town and we got chatting. To be honest, even then I could tell we didn't have much in common, but the whole 'eighties' thing is getting to me, and with my funds from these new fangled computer thingamajigs making me richer all the time, I figure I can afford to have some nymphomaniac gold-digger as a girlfriend, at least for a while.

The main reason we've come to France for a month is to escape the hell back home. Between the miner's strike and the whole 'Big Brother is watching you' mentality that's going around, I'd prefer to be here on the beach surrounded by dozens of naked hot babes any day.

Knowing the effect that finally being in Orwell's '1984' would have on the public, I decided last year to further improve my finances. I sent an idea to Channel Four suggesting that a show named *Big Brother* might be a good idea and that there was good money to be made through a cheap idea called 'reality television'. I outlined the proposal that you got non-Equity members of the general public to live together in a house for a couple of months where various 'unscripted' things happened and people voted to get rid of their least favourite characters. At the end, Channel Four would give a large sum of money to the surviving member who would also gain a large amount of totally undeserved media coverage.

In short form Channel Four, famed for showing their series of 'Red Triangle' adult or banned films featuring devil worship, lesbianism and graphic violence, wrote back the following:

Dear Sir or Madam,

Thank you for your recent submission to our new programming department entitled 'Big Brother'. Whilst we welcome input from the general public we feel that this idea lacks the artistic direction that we at Channel Four are aiming for. Perhaps you might interest the BBC or ITV with this concept, but alas, it is not for us.

Yours faithfully,
Channel 4

Which is symptomatic of the way that everything goes when I try to implement ideas from the future. Still, never one to be put off, I took a copy of my letter, sealed it, had it sworn by a solicitor and left instructions for it to be opened in the year 2000 as proof that Channel Four stole my idea, thus forming the basis of a rather lucrative future legal suit against the fledgling broadcaster.

Anyway, at this time the population of the Britain are still convinced that George Orwell was some kind of twentieth century Nostradamus and I decided that no price was too high to pay to get out of the country for a bit and get away from picket lines, power cuts and harbingers of doom.

As I sit here, basking under a crystal blue sky, staring out to sea as I watch various tanned girls bounce up and down in time with the ocean, I think back to what the younger me was doing at this time. I remember doing okay at school, being bit of a loner, bit of an outcast, always being too smug and self-righteous for my own good. I'd be nearly fourteen now and though I haven't been back to Leicester in years, I do send a birthday card to myself just to stay in touch. I suppose sometime soon I'll have to have that 'sorting your life out' talk with little Julian before everything gets too screwed up again.

And I can't believe that it's almost five years already. It seems like yesterday, that afternoon at Dave's house when everything went wrong, when it all fell apart.

It all finally hit me, the things Dave was saying, the past tense he kept using when he referred to Jenny, the heavy aura that permeated his living room, the feeling that something was far from right. When all the clues finally made their way through my half-drunk brain, I just threw up all over his sofa. All over his floor.

I just crumpled and sat there, the realisation dawning on me that something incredibly bad had happened, something that I could do nothing about. In a heartbeat my life had just been altered beyond all recognition.

Dave was a wreck. He just sat there, hunched up, rocking himself back and forth as I wiped my mouth and struggled back to my feet. I somehow made it to the hallway, up the stairs and into the bedroom.

In contrast to the squalor Dave had generated downstairs this room was immaculate, everything tidy, everything in its place. The suitcases, I noticed, were on top of the wardrobe, Jenny's things all neatly arranged around the room.

And there, where I didn't really want to look, in the bed, was Jenny. She was just lying there as if she'd gone to sleep, perfectly normal except for the nasty gash on her forehead that had spilled a little blood onto the pillow. She looked exactly as any sleeping woman would look except for the colour of her skin and the lack of even the smallest movement.

Dave had just picked her up and put her to bed, tidied the room and left her to sleep. Perhaps part of him didn't want to acknowledge the truth, perhaps he was still waiting for her to wake up and go downstairs and give him hell for making the house such a mess.

I knelt at the side of the bed, took her cold hand in mine and cried my heart out for what seemed like forever.

And when I got through the sobbing I moved on to the worst afternoon of my life.

I made Dave leave the house. I told him that whatever happened he was to just repeat the story that his wife had left him. He didn't know where she was, that he went home after being out with me and they argued and she left. I told him to go to the police in a couple of days, register her as missing.

He was panicky, but I knew he'd sort it out. I know he didn't go to prison during the eighties or nineties and I finally understood now why the father I knew, the man who raised me and my sister alone, was so subdued and quiet. I told him never to leave that house unattended, never to move. I told him I'd sort everything out.

I told him to stay away until midnight and I let him know that that this was the end of our friendship. I would sort things out, but he'd never see me again after today.

I don't know where he went, but I knew what I had to do. I went to a hardware store and bought tough plastic bags, the kind builders put masonry debris into. I got wooden panelling, screws and nails. At the back of my mind I thought it was all hopeless, that the police would easily find out what I'd done. But I also knew the future, and if it was true that nothing I did made much difference to the events to come, then I knew that this secret would be safe for at least twenty years.

I cried as I forced Jenny's body into a thick black plastic bag and sealed it up with enough tape to make it airtight. I pushed and bent her until I'd got her into the largest suitcase I could find and somehow managed to manoeuvre the case through the opening that led to the attic.

The tears and grief were on hold for a while as I busied myself clearing a space at the far end of the roof. From the panelling I made a wooden cabinet big enough to hold the suitcase, together with some of her clothes and personal effects. The whole thing was fixed to the floor and the brickwork and I nailed and glued the top into place.

And there it was. The final resting place of Jennifer Louise Grant. My mother. My lover.

I surrounded the cabinet with various boxes of old clothes and toys, and placed a few piles of books on top of it. With any luck it would remain hidden for the rest of Dave's life.

I said my final goodbyes to Jenny and I left and moved to a new flat before Dave could make contact with me. Perhaps one day I'll go back and see him, but the way I felt then and still feel now, I'd just as soon never see my father again.

And back here, on the beach at Cannes, Michelle gets up, takes a handful of francs from my wallet and informs me that she's off to find a bar.

She pulls on a neon-pink skirt and a 'Frankie Says...' T-shirt and asks why I'm looking so sad and all I can manage by way of an answer is a shrug. I tell her to bring me back a beer as she grabs her flip-flops and walks away.

Despite the peace and quiet, the sun, the sea and the naked girls all around me, my life is still totally fucked up. I'm not even sure about what I'm doing any more. I'm running from the past and the future all at once and have no real idea which direction I'm supposed to be heading in.

And don't ask how I know it, but back at home, right at this second, as I'm sitting on the beach lamenting the past, someone with a crow-bar is prying open a window and is breaking into my new flat.

1984 - 1985

It was 1985 that proved beyond a doubt that the best way to confuse the American film-going public was to slap a flux capacitor into a DeLorean sports car and start sending people backward and forward in time like there's no tomorrow.

This was the year we were introduced to Marty McFly, a seventeen year old schoolboy played by twenty-four year old Michael J Fox. Marty lives at home with his twenty-four year old mother and his twenty-one year old father, and spends a lot of his time playing the electric guitar whilst skateboarding through the streets of Hill Valley.

To save his friend, Doc Brown, Marty must go back in time to 1955, a year when his parents were still in school and all the kids are bullied by twenty-six year old student, Biff Tannen.

There is much amusement as Marty makes jokes about things that haven't been invented yet and in a bizarre and some would say morally wrong plot twist, his own mother becomes sexually attracted to him and almost wipes out all his future history.

Film-goers would be further confused by a sequel in which Marty goes to the future and meets his kids, then goes back to an alternate 1985, then back again to 1955 to put 1985 straight before finding that Doc Brown has been catapulted back through time to the nineteenth century. Mysteriously his father is now quite literally a new man and his girlfriend has been exchanged for a completely different twenty-six year old actress, not that Marty cares since he is now getting away with pretending to be seventeen, even though he is actually twenty-eight.

Thankfully, everything settles down in Part Three and it all turns into a good, old-fashioned western with ZZ Top, banjos and time-travelling trains.

13 July 1985
... And Your Chicks For Free

Pretty much everyone remembers where they were on the day *Live Aid* was broadcast to the world. I was almost fifteen years old and had cycled out to a river in a nearby village with my best mate, Colin. We were supposed to be watching the concert at his place, but his parents were arguing and Colin wanted to get out of the house so we grabbed our bikes and headed off for an afternoon of adventuring along the river to some abandoned farm buildings we hung out at from time to time.

We often went to the old farm and pretended that we owned the place and were, in our own little way, kings for the time that we were there. We used to imagine that bodies were hidden there, the mangled and decaying remains of young girls, kidnapped and tortured by insane maniacs. It all seemed so innocent back then, never giving a thought to the fact that out there in the real world, there actually were people getting tortured and killed. Just around the corner was adulthood where kids were really being kidnapped, real bombs were being set off and actual planes were getting hijacked. For us it was still all just make believe. We had nothing to fear as we roamed our private little kingdom looking for excitement.

On this particular day, at this exact time, 4.15pm, as I sit here at home watching a never ending list of stars perform for the future of Africa, my younger self is some thirty miles away, losing his virginity.

I toyed with the idea of turning up for the occasion and providing some moral support, but it seems that with every day that passes it gets more difficult for me to connect with my other life. He'll have to go through this without me and besides, I have more than enough trouble to keep me busy right now.

That day, or this day depending on how you look at it, the day I lost my virginity, was one of the strangest of my life so far. Me and Colin had made it down to the farm buildings and were about to embark on our customary body hunt when we heard voices coming from the main barn.

We crept up there, peered through a crack in the battered, wooden walls and found a couple going at it hammer and tongs on a blanket thrown down on top of a bed of old hay. Naturally, we couldn't take our eyes off the sight and took it in turns to squint through the gap and get a really obscured view of some guy's arse bobbing up and down. Truth be told, we couldn't see a thing. The girl was pretty much fully clothed and the bloke had his trousers round his ankles as they panted, moaned and occasionally yelled out seemingly random obscenities.

Still, it was better entertainment than the porno mags we'd managed to get our hands on from time to time and far easier than the occasions I'd tried to catch Colin's older sister, Rebecca, in the shower. Sadly for the two unwitting performers, as the bloke charged toward his climax, either me or Colin slipped, knocked over some loose bricks and generally made enough noise to wake the dead, let alone put a young couple off their shagging.

The next thing we knew the guy was standing over us, thankfully with his pants pulled up, and half-embarrassed, half angry, asked us what the fuck we thought we were doing spying on him. For a very real moment I had the irrational fear that he was going to torture us, kill us and hide our bodies in the barn.

Stuck for words we just stared at our feet until eventually the girl, who it turns out we both knew from school, poked her head round the barn door.

Her name was Sally Heller, infamous around the playground for being sexually active at fourteen and well known for doing it with blokes in exchange for fags and booze. Though 'prostitute' was a bit of a harsh phrase for someone her age, it was nevertheless a pretty appropriate one.

"I know you!" Colin chirped up, and I realised he wasn't talking to Sally, but to the bloke. "You're that new teacher who's taking over our physics class when Mrs Dyer leaves!"

It was news to me, but then I'd been skipping one or two classes lately. It must have been true though, because the guy went bright red and flustered about uncontrollably. He could see his whole future career crashing down before his eyes accompanied by news headlines in *The Sun* declaring him to be the newly crowned 'Kiddie-Fiddler of the Year'.

"You can't tell anyone about this!" He almost stammered out the words. "I'll lose my job!"

Me and Colin looked at each other, realisation dawning on us that at that moment we wielded more power than at any other time in our relatively young lives. "What's it worth?" I asked him.

Mr Keanes, as I later found out was his name, became overwhelmed and stuttered and just couldn't manage to find the words to answer me. Eventually it was Sally who suggested that if we kept our mouths shut she'd let us both have sex with her, provided we also gave her five pounds each.

We pooled our pocket money, realised that it would take us a few weeks to save up the whole ten quid, struck a deal for a pound each for the next five weeks and each in turn disappeared into the barn whilst the other one kept Mr Keanes company.

Needless to say we both blew our loads in record time and were heading back down the riverside to home in less than ten minutes. I recall that Sally Heller didn't even show us her tits which, if I'd been a better negotiator, I would have included in the whole 'five quid each' deal.

Mr Keanes, with whom I'd had a fascinating discussion about next year's syllabus whilst Colin had his go with Sally, didn't turn up for school at the beginning of the next term. He'd apparently put in for a transfer to somewhere far, far away stating that he had 'personal reasons' for making the move. Sally Heller spent the next year getting rich off sexual favours before she was taken out of school on account of a 'mystery illness' that bore all the hallmarks of a teenage pregnancy.

Meanwhile, back in my current life, as the younger me is getting laid and Status Quo are rocking all over the world, I've got more pressing problems that need to be dealt with. Problems going by the names of Pete and Diane.

When I was on holiday last year down in Cannes, Pete managed to track me down and casually let himself and Diane into my flat. When I returned home with Michelle I found that he'd managed to turn my newly decorated little home into a landfill site. And all I got by way of explanation was a quick, "Hello, Jules, how have you been?"

It turns out that having finally been let out of prison in 1978, Pete, in desperate need of an income, went straight back to his political-activist-for-hire ways and made himself available to fight for whichever cause paid the most cash. He claimed responsibility for many of the bombings of the past few years, though how much is gospel and how much is bullshit I've yet to find out.

Whilst working on a job in the North he put out some feelers and traced Diane, now separated from Viv, who had settled down quite nicely and was working as a hairdresser.

Diane had turned her back on her same-sex relationship ways, had grown her hair back and seemed to be getting along quite well on her own until the sudden arrival one day of Pete, about four years ago. With all the charm of a drunken pit bull, Pete had strolled into her shop and ordered that she accompany him on a life of extravagance, debauchery and general mayhem.

He must have made a persuasive argument and for whatever her personal reasons Diane agreed and they teamed up, got married and soon had a reputation for being the best husband and wife mercenary team north of Watford.

Last year, on the run from some quite intense police investigations, they headed south and started looking up old contacts. Somehow I came out on top of their list of places to lie low and consequently, when I returned from the South of France, I found both of them asleep in my bed and the kitchen was filled with more dirty crockery than I knew I owned.

They claimed it just temporary, until the heat died down from some botched job they were on in Huddersfield. They were, according to Pete, supposed to go to the home of a bank manager, gun him down and leave a note from some terrorist organisation I've never heard of admitting responsibility for the murder. Somehow, and Pete clearly blames Diane for this, they got the wrong house and shot dead a vicar who was minding his own business, sleeping the sleep of the righteous. To make matters worse the bank manager had got wind of the hit, went into hiding and now both the police and the obscure terrorists were gunning for them. It appears that Pete took fifty thousand pounds for the job and they'd rather like it back.

So they found my current address a year ago and have been lurking in my spare room, eating my food, watching my TV and spending what seems like twelve hours a day either sleeping or shagging ever since. On the plus side, at least it's keeping them out of trouble.

The thing is, there doesn't seem to be any hint that they might move out and they're really starting to get in the way of any meaningful relationships I might want to nurture. Michelle buggered off the day after we got back from Cannes, and other girls I've brought home have found it a bit off-putting when we're watching a nice girly, touchy-feely video and I'm about to make my move and Dave wanders through, stark-bollock naked, to fetch himself a drink from the kitchen.

It's definitely getting to the point where some severe words will have to be said.

1985 – 1986

The world of computing changes once more as Microsoft launches the innovative Windows operating system. Although still working alongside the standard DOS operating system, the Windows package would allow computer users to multitask and better organise their work. Later versions of the software would add to this functionality and, when coupled with word processing and spreadsheets, would radically alter the way individuals and businesses conducted their day-to-day tasks.

Over the years Windows has become the world's standard computer operating system and it's easy to see why, particularly in the office environment.

Firstly, the ability to quickly 'flick' between different 'windows' means it is much easier for staff to play Solitaire or Minesweeper and mask the game with a letter or a spreadsheet when the boss walks into the room. This clearly saves a huge amount of management time on disciplinary lectures and bollockings.

Secondly, and more importantly, the graphical nature of the Windows interface meant it was the ideal medium for sharing and downloading images, especially pornography. Following its launch, the development of the Internet was actually speeded up to ensure a steady flow of porn around the world. Indeed, amendments to the US constitution are currently being considered to ensure that every computer user is presented with at least one image of a nude body every ten minutes, with no regard to which site you are actually browsing.

In some states this recommendation is already being surpassed whilst in Germany it is now mandatory to have a large cock appear on your screen at least once every thirty seconds.

26 April 1986
... No Plastic Money Anymore

My frustration with living in the past is really starting to get to me.

This total inability to change events, to know the future and yet be nothing more than a spectator, is enough to drive any man insane. Earlier this year I wrote to NASA, warning them that the Challenger shuttle wouldn't be space worthy when it launched. I got no reply and the shuttle blew up, taking its place in history exactly as I remember it. Today, the nuclear reactor at Chernobyl went into meltdown, irradiating large areas of Russia for years to come. Again, the countless warnings I sent fell on deaf ears.

I'm beginning to wonder if I should ever actually bother meeting my younger self. I mean, what is the point if nothing I do changes anything? But then again, maybe small things can be altered, maybe on a personal level I can still make some sort of difference, perhaps it's just global events I can do nothing about.

But does any of it really matter? I have nothing else to do and it looks like I'm destined to live in my own past until whatever force that sent me here deems it the right time to send me home. In all probability I think I'm expected to stay here until 2006 when I suppose my life will get back on track and I'll be able to learn something from all these experiences.

At least, that's this year's theory.

It's like being trapped in a production of *A Christmas Carol* and I'm playing the part of Ebenezer Scrooge, but the Ghost of Christmas Past has buggered off, leaving me to sort things out by myself. Though if really pushed, I must admit that some of it has been fun and the past sixteen years have practically flown by.

Speaking of fun, Pete and Diane are still hanging around, they've been squatting with me now for almost two years and whilst they still seem to spend a ridiculous amount of time in bed, at least they've started clearing up after themselves and on a few occasions I've even caught Diane washing their dirty dishes.

I've often toyed with the idea of calling in the police to get rid of them, but I'm not sure that's a particularly good idea since Pete isn't the sort of person you really want carrying a grudge against you. Sure I'd get rid of him for now, but in five, ten, fifteen years he'll get released and I'll be at the top of his list of people he'd dreamed of killing every night during his stay in prison.

So I continue to put up with them and, as I sit in my living room, watching the *Nine O'clock News*' coverage of the reactor disaster, Diane quietly walks in, closes the door and sits down on the sofa.

She puts a finger to her lips and whispers, "He's asleep."

I nod and turn the volume down on TV. It's all old news to me anyway.

Diane looks tired, which is quite a feat for someone who spends as much time sleeping as she does.

"Jules," she whispers, "I need to ask a favour."

"Anything for you. Does it involve helping you and Pete move to a new house?"

She either deliberately ignores me or just doesn't care. She actually seems to be quite nervous. "A big favour."

I sit quietly, waiting for her to elaborate.

"I'm getting worried about Pete. I think he's losing it. He's sleeping all the time, only awake for maybe four or five hours a day. I think he's ill or something. When he wakes up all he talks about is this one last job he wants to do. He just lies there and tells me he wants to go out with a bang."

I have to admit that, now I think about it, I haven't seen much of Pete for the past couple of months. I just let him get on with things, more than happy that I could get back some semblance of order without him interfering in my life all the time. It's hardly headline news that he's losing the plot, as far as I can tell he's not been right in the head since I met him in 1970. Last time I saw him he didn't look particularly ill, though if nothing else, Pete is a man with many secrets.

"I'm worried that he'll take me down with him. If he's got some sort of death wish then I don't want to be a part of it. I need to get away, but wherever I go Pete will follow me."

"He can't force you to do anything you don't want to." Which is nothing if not a meaningless platitude as I'm more than certain that Pete is capable of forcing anyone to do whatever he wants.

"Jules, I'm scared. You'll think I'm mad, but I'm sure he's going to kill me."

She's been living here for nearly two years and in all that time we've had just a handful of conversations. Usually it was 'Does anyone want anything from the shop?' or 'Whose is this thing at the back of the fridge?' It seemed a fairly big jump for her to move straight on to 'Hi Jules, Pete's going to kill me.'

"If I leave him, he'll come after me. If I stay here I think he'll force me to die with him."

Pete was always unbalanced, but things seem to be getting out of control. I'm a little ashamed to admit that I've been living with the guy for ages now and haven't picked up on any of this.

"So what did you have in mind?"

"I've still got money from that bank manager job, about ten thousand that Pete thinks I've spent. I'll share it with you if you help me kill him."

I'm wondering at which point I'd fallen asleep and started dreaming all this up. "*Kill him?* You and Me? Kill Pete?" I was stumbling a little, but I think I managed to get out all the salient points.

"It's the only way. It's not like you'd be doing anything major since he's dying anyway."

"I think you'll find the police don't look at things in quite that simple a light. And do you actually know for a fact that he's dying? Perhaps he's just ill?" There were instantly about a hundred reasons jumping around my head for why this was all an incredibly bad idea. "You can't seriously expect me to kill someone! I thought you were supposed to be the hardened, anything-for-cash terrorist."

She shakes her head. "I can't kill him. I'm still in love him. I just don't want to die with him."

"And you think I can do it instead? Don't you have 'friends' that deal with this sort of stuff?"

"We made more enemies than friends over the years. Why do you think I'm asking you? We go back so far. Remember all those meetings we went to in Steve's bedroom?"

"I hardly think that classes us as best buddies! And since you came back into my life I've seen precious little of either of you! You break into my flat while I'm on holiday, eat my food, use all my hot water, Pete scares away all my girlfriends and you both keep me awake half the night whilst you go at each other like particularly noisy rabbits! I don't think I've missed out anything major. Were there any other things you do for me that fall into the 'stuff friends do for each other' category?"

My spine suddenly chills as Pete's voice carries over from the now open door.

"She forgot to mention that I've got two suitcases full of explosives under the bed. And my plan is that we three mates all head down to London, find the biggest crowds we can and blow ourselves up. I was just going to take Diane and make it one of those tragic 'lovers joint suicide' things, but now I'm afraid I'll have to take you along too. A *ménage a trois* if you will. Oh, and she's right, I am dying. I have a month, maybe two. Plenty of time to track you both down if you try and run out on me."

Diane was right about one thing. Pete was totally stark-raving bonkers. "What the hell do you think you're planning to do, Pete?"

"I'm dying, Julian. I'm leaving this pathetic little world behind and I want to take as many people with me as I can."

"Including your wife?"

"It wasn't in my original plan, but she's becoming a liability. I don't want her tarnishing my saintly image after I'm gone."

"And me?"

"You know too much now. I can hardly let you live."

"So now you're some kind of James Bond villain? You're insane, Pete! You are aware of that, aren't you? You do realise that normal, sane people don't act this way?"

Pete just stands there in the doorway. He's naked again and I'm not entirely sure that he's worn any clothes for months now. "I know. It's kind of liberating. I don't have all those shitty morals running around my head telling me who I should or shouldn't be hurting. The voices just tell me to kill everyone."

Which, joke or not, really isn't the answer you want to hear when you've just found out that there's a maniac in your house with two suitcases of explosives tucked away under your spare bed. Christ! Just how long have I been sleeping in the same house as two suitcases filled with dynamite?

And now I'm faced with the reality of actually having to incapacitate Pete, which might get taken the wrong way by the police if I accidentally kill him. However, if I do nothing, the insane bastard is going to kill us both either before or during his proposed trip to London.

"How mad would you say I am, Diane?" he says, stepping fully into the living room and starting to rub himself. "Mad enough to hurt you if you don't do exactly what I say?" And the mental case just stands there, between me and her, waving his growing erection in her face.

Just ten minutes ago I was watching the news and wondering about getting myself some cheese on toast before heading to bed. Now, I'm in fear for my life and looking around the room, looking at the coffee table beside me and thinking 'scissors'. I'm thinking back to that afternoon at Dave's house. Potential weapons are lying around everywhere.

"Suck it, Diane." He's saying and she takes his cock in her hand and, scared of the consequences, starts to rub it. He's like a man possessed. He's in a world where he makes all the rules and everyone else exists only to do his bidding. And as Diane lowers her mouth, I grab the scissors, pull them open and I'm out of my seat, plunging a blade straight into the base of Pete's neck.

With a less effort than I expected the stainless steel spike goes straight in and then up, barely stopping on the bones in his neck. Pete spins round, gurgling, blood coming from his lips as he gasps and lets me see the glint of metal that's protruding from the inside of his mouth.

As he crashes against the wall and slides to the floor Diane is on her feet again, trembling and looking at her husband as he thrashes out his last moments.

I'm wondering how she's going to react. I've just killed her husband which, granted, was exactly what she had asked me to do, but I'm not too sure that this is the way she wanted it to happen. She would have probably opted for an alternative to the 'scissors in the neck, blood spraying everywhere' plan.

Pete's just lying there, staring at Diane, sputtering through his last breaths as his wife walks up to him and, just once, smacks her foot into his crotch.

"Useless fucker!"

Is all she says.

And as I watch the pool of blood around Pete slowly grow, Diane quietly heads into the spare room and starts packing.

1986 – 1987

Many people will fondly remember this as the year that Star Trek returned to our screens in the exciting, new *Next Generation* format. No more Kirk and Spock, no more brightly coloured red, blue and yellow corridors. This was all-new *Trek*. This was elderly captains with no hair, pyjama jumpsuits for all and pastel-pink decor.

Boldly re-writing the most popular scripts from the original series, The Next Generation lasted for seven seasons and four movies before finally laying down its phasers for good and standing aside to let that guy from Quantum Leap finish everything off for good.

But it wasn't all space exploration and Klingons off the starboard bow.

Back on Earth the TV watching public are treated to *Married ... With Children* and each week we are shown just how amusing a dysfunctional American family could be. We would laugh as the indolent father, Al Bundy, moved his toilet into the living room and howl as his wife, Peggy, tried every means possible to get her hands on Al's hard earned cash. What everyone did when Christina Applegate turned up jiggling around in a skimpy bikini is their own perfectly justified, personal, private business.

Sadly, despite my sending in the finished screenplay more than a dozen times, the Fox Network turned down my idea for an end of series finale where Al's father, Ted Bundy, comes to visit and the whole female cast are violently raped and murdered in their sleep. Not quite what they were after, they said.

Meanwhile, also on Fox, another dysfunctional family of strangely drawn cartoon characters were just getting started...

15 October 1987
... Maybe It's Because I'm Crazy

Lately I've been having recurring dreams about Jenny. In my dreams she appears out of nowhere, alive, healthy and happy. She comes and finds me to tell me how much she's missing me, that she knows the truth about who I am but doesn't care. We touch, we hug and every time I try to tell her how I feel she vanishes without a trace.

Almost every night now, for the last month or so.

I expect tonight will be no different. Tonight is that hurricane thing, the one that causes more damage to the south-east than any storm in history but that the weathermen never saw coming. Apparently someone sent in a letter to them warning them that a storm was coming and they just brushed it away. This time it isn't me. And it's quite reassuring to see that it's not just me that gets ignored all the time.

Up here in the Midlands the storm isn't so bad, but the wind is rattling the glass in the windows and some of the trees look as if they might come down given half an excuse. It's three in the morning and I can't sleep. Jenny keeps threatening to haunt me every time I close my eyes.

Every so often I think of Dave, living out each day unaware that his wife's body is hidden in his attic. Hopefully it hasn't been found, I don't remember any talk of a body in the roof back in the future so there's no reason that it should have been.

I stand in front of the window and look down on the street below where a bin has blown over, its contents dancing wildly in the gusting air. The rain batters against the glass and a house over the road has lost its 'For Sale' board from the garden.

By morning there'll be a host of cars with branches through their windscreen and dustbins lying on their sides with stray cats feasting on the leftovers that have fallen out. I suddenly remember a story about some guy down south waking up tomorrow morning and finding a Volkswagen Beatle lying on its roof in his living room.

And when I turn back from the bedroom window, with the orange glare from the street lamps lighting the walls, she's there on the bed and I know that I've finally gone mad. I've totally lost the plot. There's no way on Earth that I'm asleep.

She's there, her legs drawn up to her chin, wearing her favourite blue satin nightie and the silver heart pendant that I bought her for her birthday back when Dave was in prison and we'd first started seeing each other.

"Jen?"

She smiles, a look I'd forgotten about these past few years, the smile she had when we were first together. "Hi, Julian. Miss me?"

I know deep down that this can't be happening, that she's a phantom, something my head has conjured up to show me that I need to deal with the feelings I'm still hiding from myself. I have to accept the possibility that I've fallen asleep and this is all a dream, but right now I don't care. I just want to hold her, to fall asleep with her in my arms.

Just like things used to be.

"You went away." I tell her, still keeping my distance. I don't want to touch her and shatter the illusion. "You left me alone."

"I couldn't help it. I needed to say my goodbyes. I couldn't just vanish and leave Dave with no explanation."

I catch sight of my reflection in a mirror hanging above the mantelpiece. I look terrible, like I haven't slept in days. I look at Jen, reflected beside my face. "I always thought you left him. The family always said you moved away, left dad for someone else."

She goes back to wearing her all too familiar, sad and tired face. "And now you know the truth. There was someone else in my life, there was you. I would have gone anywhere with you, my love. But you can't change anything. Things have to happen the way they always happened, they have to unfold the way they always have."

I sit down on the bed and pull her to me, she's warm and soft and she's everything that's missing from my life right now. We slip under the sheets and she snuggles up close, her head resting on my chest.

"I never loved anyone the way I loved you." I tell her, stroking her hair. "The girls I've seen since you died, they were nothing. I never really loved them. I think most of my relationships broke down from sheer boredom on my part. Maybe I threw in a little apathy for good measure."

"You have to let me go. There are more important things for you to do. Little Julian will need you soon."

She's telling me things I already know, after all she's constructed from my own hopes and memories, subconscious dreams finding their way to the surface of my mind. My younger self will be in more trouble soon than he's ever been in before and I have to be there for him. I know this. Jenny knows this.

I think of Dave, my father, bringing up my sister and me, every day plagued by the memory of what he did to his wife, the guilt steadily rising, all bottled up inside him, always repressed. And as little Julian got older, how much more painful would it have been if I was still around? His similarity to me would have become more and more obvious, the clear, though incorrect, conclusion would be drawn that he was not Dave's son, but mine. It would have been enough to break my father. Enough to make him a pale shadow of the man I first met. I remember him being so quiet, so sober and restrained. He must have wanted to lash out in anger and desperation so many times.

And here I am now, cheating on him again in my dreams. Lying here with his wife, alive and well, still thirty years old. The woman he mourns for every day is haunting me and not him.

And tomorrow the storms will be over, tomorrow the sky will be clear and everything will be back to normal. Jenny will be gone and I will be alone again.

"Jay, I've missed you so much!" She says, telling me exactly what I need to hear. "Just hold me."

And I do. It doesn't matter that she isn't real. I hold on to her, tracing imaginary lines on her arm with my fingertips. I hold her to me and stroke her hair until she falls asleep.

The mother I never had.

The lover I couldn't hold on to.

We drift into sleep in each other's arms just like old times and just like back then, back when she was alive, I know that in the morning she'll be gone.

1987 – 1988

A third term in power begins for Mrs Thatcher's Conservative Party and, worried about the threat to human existence caused by the outbreak of HIV and AIDS, the government implements the Section 28 law reform.

Some may have thought that a clever move at this time would be to implement better awareness of the dangers of unprotected sex through the media and through sex education classes in our school systems. Clearly that would have been insane. This is, after all, Britain, the last bastion of Empire in the western world. We can't have our children learning about homosexual urges in school when they should be getting taught good, old-fashioned Victorian values.

Following in the footsteps of the great Anita Bryant, British law was changed to prevent schools and other government funded organisations from promoting or supporting homosexuality. No gay books in school libraries, no talk of botty-sex in the classroom. School sex education lessons would have to continue being opportunities to snigger as the teacher showed everyone how to put a condom on a cucumber, (which was apparently a common form of foreplay in the mid-eighties).

Section 28 brought with it media hype and public panic, but thankfully, in the fifteen years that it was in effect before being repealed it was used to bring only one case to court. The Christian Institute moved against Glasgow City Council for funding an AIDS support group which was clearly trying to turn everyone gay. That's the compassion of Christianity for you.

Like Jesus always said, back in the olden days, "They don't like it up 'em, Sir. They don't like it up 'em."

25 June 1988
... And He Packs His Lunch in a Sunblest Bag

My repeating bad dreams got fewer and less intense over time, though they never quite faded altogether and every month or so I would close my eyes and fall asleep only to find Jenny waiting for me on the other side. It was always the same theme, with me apologising for everything and Jenny telling me that things were all going the way they were always destined to have gone. The guilt never quite lets go of me though, and there's still a little voice at the back of my head that never stops telling me that I was the one responsible for Jenny's death.

I was beginning to suspect that the reasons for me being in my own past were never going to be made clear and, not wanting to regress to the mess I was in when Jenny died, I threw myself into my work at the pub. I took on extra shifts and though I rarely needed the money these days, it was good to spend as much time as possible around people who weren't going quietly insane. I even managed to hold down a couple of monogamous relationships, one of them for nearly three weeks.

Then, about two weeks ago, me and Duty Manager Bob were sitting around the bar after closing time and he said something that seemed fairly innocuous, but turned out to be one of those world-view changing events.

"Jay," he said, grabbing a bottle of scotch and a couple of glasses from behind the bar, "do you believe in fate?"

I raised an eyebrow and wondered where he was going with this. Normally, our after-hours discussions centred around which new barmaid we both wanted to sleep with or when we were going to give up bar-work all together and get proper jobs.

"You mean, is it predestined that you and me are going to serve drinks for the rest of our lives and never find true love?"

He poured the scotch and passed one to me. "I suppose I was wondering something like that. Is there more to life? Do I actually have a purpose besides collecting the biggest stash of porn-mags known to man?"

Then I remembered.

"You're thirty next week, aren't you?"

"Yeah."

"I know how it feels. When I turned thirty I spent a week reading a book of Buddhist scripture in the desperate hope of finding the meaning of life. It didn't help any. And in spite of everything I've learned since then I have less of a clue why I'm here now than I ever did."

Bob put his feet up on the table and tilted back in his chair. "A couple of years ago, I thought I'd sorted it all out."

"How come?"

"Remember Wendy? The welsh girl who used to come in and drink pints of vodka."

I remembered Wendy all right. She came in one night looking for Bob when Bob was off sick. She hung around and ended up going home with me where we spent hours and hours doing things that were probably illegal in most civilised countries. And she made me video tape the whole thing.

"Was she the blonde with enormous tits?"

"No. Brunette. Looked like Winona Ryder."

That was the one.

Bob stared into his glass.

"She was into all this weird, spiritual stuff, like meditation and chanting. She used to come over and spend hours with me contemplating life and finding inner peace. Then we'd have the most incredible sex! Afterwards, I felt that nothing in the world could touch me. That Wendy and me would be together for always and be eternally happy. I felt so ... restful."

"Bob?"

"Yes?"

"I think I know what you're talking about. Some people claim it doesn't exist, but are you are familiar with what we in the business call 'the male orgasm'?"

Bob grinned back at me. "I know! I know! But it all seemed so right at the time! With Wendy it wasn't just a case of blowing my load then phoning her a taxi. I wanted to spend forever with her!"

Well she did look a lot like Winona Ryder. Sounded more like Windsor Davies, but looked like a million dollars. I'd have been tempted to see her regularly except I really didn't want to go behind Bob's back. Well, no more than I already had done.

"So where's Wendy now?"

"She moved to Cardiff to make Welsh porn films. She sends me one of them every now and then. I'm not sure how I'm supposed to take that, I mean, how many guys have their ex sending back videos of them getting shafted up the arse by Evans the Cock's trouser snake?"

Ah yes, the Welsh porn industry. Only last week I was re-watching my own contribution, the cleverly entitled, *Wendy Takes a Leek*. It's an undisputed masterpiece of its time and I can't wait until DVD is invented so I can have it transferred to disk with a remastered 5.1 surround sound porn-music soundtrack and interactive menus.

"So, how does Wendy's defection to the self abuse industry affect your outlook on a perfect life?"

"I don't know. I try and look at everything like it's supposed to happen for a reason, that everything that goes wrong in life goes wrong so that I can learn from it."

I was back to my 'nodding sagely' routine. "And Wendy leaving you to be filmed with well-endowed Welshmen means what?"

"I think she left me so I could meet someone else."

"Which explains the number of barmaids you've been getting though recently."

"I just haven't found the right one yet."

More drinks were poured and Bob started staring out of the window at stars that were barely visible beyond the sodium glare of the streetlights.

"It's okay." I told him. "I'm sure Fate will sort you out eventually. Though you have to realise that there's a high probability that Fate is just a load of bollocks, a means for you to absolve yourself of all responsibility for your own actions."

"You were destined to say that."

"Bollocks."

But he might have been right. Back here in the past, everything was happening along its pre-ordained route. Who can say if that route ends in 2006 or if even then I'm just acting out a script? It's like watching a film. The first time round, I don't know how it's going to end, but I can't change the way that it does. It's only on the second watching that things seem predestined. Only the second time around that you know you can't stop the main character from following a course of events that will end in either happiness or disaster. That line of thought never leaves me feeling particularly happy.

"So what's your plan, Bob? Turn thirty and go through another twenty or so barmaids until you find the right one?"

"Who says it has to be a barmaid?"

"Fate, Bob. Fate has a barmaid put aside somewhere especially for you. Maybe you and that Katrina are destined to get it together?"

"I don't think so!"

"Why not? If that's what Fate has planned for you, there's nothing you can do about it!"

"One of her eyes points in a funny direction!"

"There's nothing that funny about looking up and to the right."

"There is when the other one is staring at me like I'm her next meal!"

"Fate made that happen! Fate has made her attracted to you. This time next year she could be Mrs Bob!"

And I got up, patted Bob on the shoulder and grabbed my coat. "I'm off home! Forget all this 'Fate' business! Just go through life and do what comes naturally. Start thinking too hard and you'll go mad. Even if you're supposed to do something, you won't know about it until after it's done and you're left dealing with the fallout."

And just like that, I solved all of my own problems.

As I headed to the main door of the pub, I finally realised that all these years of worrying had counted for bugger-all and that whether I was fated to do things or not, I'd have ended up at this exact same spot. All I had to do was take care of the minor, day-to-day problems and let life happen at its own pace.

I waved goodnight to Bob, wished him every happiness with his future wife, Katrina the cross-eyed barmaid and flagged down a taxi home.

1988 – 1989

Another decade draws to a close and George Herbert Walker Bush is voted in as the 41st President of the United States. George hails from a prestigious family of Georges, including his grandfather, George Herbert Walker, his uncle, George Herbert Walker II and his cousin, George Herbert Walker III.

George has a son, George Walker Bush, who would go on to do something or other in the US government whilst polishing up his innate ability for public speaking. Fortunately, George Junior is generally referred to as George W Bush, thus preventing any confusion with his father, George W Bush.

On the other side of the Atlantic, Britain was celebrating the end of free speech with the publication of The Satanic Verses, the fourth novel by Indian-born writer, Salman Rushdie.

Following the book's publication a number of Islamic organisations got a bit steamed up and ordered several book burnings until the publisher decided to withdraw it from print and pulp all remaining copies. Around the world, shops are firebombed and organised riots cause the death and injury of hundreds of people.

Various countries impose prison sentences and fines for possession of the book and shortly before his death, Ayatollah Khomeini issues a fatwa ordering all Muslims to ensure the deaths of all those involved in the publication of the novel and commanding his followers to send Rushdie himself to Hell.

Which I'm sure is all perfectly reasonable behaviour.

The bounty on Rushdie's head is currently said to be some $2.8 million and Iran has recently confirmed that since a fatwa can only be withdrawn by the person who issued it, the death sentence will remain in effect forever.

25 August 1989
... We Are Agents of the Free

Life goes on and as the weather has been quite good recently, I've organised a day-trip out for the regulars and staff of the *Old Bell*.

The destination was democratically put to the vote and for some totally inexplicable reason seventy-eight percent of the alcoholic wasters wanted to go to Skegness where the sky is perpetually grey, the North Sea is interminably cold and no matter what time of year you go there, it will, at some point, rain.

But that's the beauty of democracy for you and since I'd foolishly let the votes be counted by Bernard and Clarence, I couldn't now rig the result without disposing of both of them first. And Clarence is notoriously difficult to get your hands on.

So, only mildly put off by the fact that my own suggestion of a daytrip to Amsterdam gained only ten percent of the vote, I booked the coach and we found ourselves standing in the early morning chill, waiting for it to turn up and take us on a ride of excitement to the jewel of the east coast.

Twenty of us are foolish enough to head off this morning, and Bernard has appointed himself as Head of Operations and put himself in charge of making sure that everyone has a good time in a totally militaristic fashion. Although the trip was my idea, I'm quite happy for Bernard to do all the actual shepherding work since I'm only really here for appearances sake and would much rather be in Amsterdam. Or in bed for that matter. Plus it's not like he has to do it alone since he's got Clarence for company and, while they take the gang round the amusement arcades and along the beach, I'll hopefully get some time alone with Diane, who, since Pete's rather sudden departure from the world, has returned to Nottingham and taken rather a shine to me. I'm hoping that maybe we'll get chance to be alone someplace quiet.

The strangest thing is that, since the dreams of Jenny have pretty much stopped, I actually find myself wanting to make things really work out with Diane. I find myself wanting to spend time with her, finding out things about her, not rushing her for sex and considering her feelings. And although I know that she has bisexual tendencies and it turns me on immensely, I don't even mention it to her when we're out on dates. For the first time in almost a decade I'm getting to be all considerate and caring. We must be fast approaching the nineties.

A roll-call of passengers later and in no particular order we have Diane and myself, Bernard and Clarence, Bob, Simon, Kelly and Fiona, all bar staff along for the ride, Hamilton and his young ward Richard, a couple I've never seen before called Scott and Rachael, and regular drinkers Paul, Nigel, Adrian, Clive, Bill and Katie, who will probably just find a pub somewhere and do what they normally do, but a hundred miles away from home.

Finally there are Brian and Helen, the latest landlord and landlady of the pub. Add to that motley bunch Kevin, the driver who is paid simply to drive and keep his mouth shut and we're all on our way to the adventure capital of the world.

We arrive in the mighty Skeg at nine-thirty and since it's still fairly early the streets are reasonably empty and everyone piles off the bus and runs down to the beach to feel the sand beneath their feet and do a bit of paddling.

Everyone here knows Skegness like the back of their hands, having been here every other year on family holidays when they were kids and then coming back again on day trips like these throughout their adult lives. Even so, Bernard still hands out maps to everyone and lets them know the emergency procedures should there be any accidents, mishaps or declarations of world war three. Within minutes everyone is being marched off down the beach on their specially constructed itinerary which will take in all the major landmarks and finally, hopefully, end up at a pub somewhere.

At the first stopping-off point, the statue of the fat, prancing figure of 'The Jolly Fisherman', the icon of Skegness, Bernard has already lost a quarter of the party to the amusement arcades and I wander over to give him a bit of encouragement.

"Look after the troops, Bernie." I say, patting him on the back. "You're a good leader and, although you're losing a few of your men, I know you won't fail. You're not the kind of man who falls short of his goals."

Giving him an extra pat on the head for good luck I leave him to it and me and Diane head off into the Skegness back streets to find somewhere that's serving breakfasts.

"Skegness in the summertime!" she says to me as we push open the door of the auspiciously named *'Bev's Cafe'*. "Wonderful!"

And she smiles, which she's been doing a lot of lately. I don't remember her doing that very much when I knew her in Leicester or when she was squatting in my flat. Since she finally managed to break free of Pete she's been more confident, less stressed and if anything more beautiful than I ever remember seeing her before. But then, I'm fast becoming more than a little biased. Which worries me a bit.

We had that conversation again last night, the one where she tells me she just wants us to stay friends and not mess it up with the whole 'relationship' angle, and I nodded and agreed and told her not to worry, once again confirming that I wasn't pushing her for anything more than she wanted to give.

The final votes are yet to be counted, but there appears to be a growing certainty that I might be falling in love.

The cafe we've chosen is a typical seaside town 'greasy spoon' with net curtains to show how classy it is and my, don't we look just like quaint, old-fashioned tea rooms, and everything is covered with blue-checked, plastic tablecloths for that easy-wipe functionality. We sit down and a waitress wanders over and takes our order. I go for an orange juice and full English with chips, Diane has a pot of coffee with the double egg and chips.

Pure Skegness culinary poetry.

"So," I ask, "enjoying the day so far?"

"Oh yes! It might have been improved if Nigel hadn't thrown up on the journey here, but otherwise, absolutely wonderful!"

There's a glint in her eye that says she's happy and that this could have been anywhere in the world and things couldn't be better. I make another of my mental notes to stop staring at her like a loon and remember that she just wants to be friends and I realise I'm grinning at her again and she takes my hand in hers and shakes her head and our drinks are unceremoniously dropped in front of us, ruining the moment, but she's still smiling and looking gorgeous and we just sit there in silence smiling at each other until the food turns up and I finally remember to breathe again.

As I'm tucking into a sausage, she's slicing into her eggs and she looks at me and says, "I was thinking about the things we said last night."

And my heart plummets because, time and again, she feels she has to make this point and that somehow she thinks, probably quite rightly, that I won't give up until we've gone too far and ruined a perfectly good friendship. "I told you not to worry. I'm more than happy sharing times like these with you. The last thing in the world I want is to push you into something you're not ready for."

She puts her knife and fork down at the side of her plate and I get the feeling that this isn't quite the right time to have a mouthful of bacon and beans, so I put my cutlery down too and awkwardly swallow my food.

"I know you want more than this."

"More than breakfast in Skegness? Don't talk stupid!"

"No, more than 'just good friends'."

"You don't have to go through all this again." This line of conversation will just bring me down and I don't want to spoil how I'm feeling today. "I told you I'd keep my feelings for you under control."

"You aren't doing a very good job of that at the minute!" There's no hint of anger in her voice.

"Well you keep looking at me and smiling!" And she looks. She smiles. And I give in and shovel a load of still too-hot chips into my mouth to distract me.

"Last night, I was wrong."

And I almost choke as two of the chips I'm munching on try to get sucked down my windpipe.

"I'm making excuses. I'm protecting myself from threats that aren't there." She looks at me so sweetly and I notice for the first time how green her eyes are. "You're not Pete and I can't stop myself being happy just in case I get hurt again. And here, today, in all this," she gestures at the cafe, at the net curtains, at the blue, plastic tablecloths, "I can't stop myself being happy anyway."

"So does this mean...?"

"It means I'll get in deeper, maybe over my head, but I think that it's a risk I need to take."

"Diane..."

"Ask me to marry you and it's all off again."

"Ah." I pause. I look at her, at those oh, so green eyes, "Your chips are getting cold."

All day we wandered the beach, under the pier, over the shale, once I even skipped through the sea and got my boots and socks soaked. To an outside observer it must have all looked rather sickening and possibly a bit deranged.

We held hands, we told stories of previous visits to Skegness, of family holidays and other places we'd been to. She told me how, when she was seven, her parents inherited a little money and had taken her to Disneyland in California and she'd met Mickey Mouse. I told her of the time I went to Great Yarmouth and my dad made us dig nuclear blast holes in the beach. Next to her story, it sounded a bit crappy so I told her of the time I went to Paris and how beautiful I'd found the city.

It was sickening, but I hadn't felt like this for so long. I'd forgotten what it was like. I'd spent so much time in love with a memory, running from a ghost, that I'd almost missed this opportunity to be happy.

And eventually, as the first spots of rain fall on our day, we head over to the *Parrot and Perch* where most of the group are likely to be hiding out, drinking whilst waiting for Bernard to get back with the ones that made it through the whole guided tour intact.

And we're half way through our third pint and Nigel is just starting his latest rendition of *American Pie* and suddenly Hamilton bursts through the pub door with all the strength his frail, ninety year-old body can manage and in a cracked and aged voice yells out, "Trouble! On the Beach! Bernard!"

And the whole group rushes out to stand at the railings, staring in horror at what's happening on the sea front.

There's a small crowd watching, half of them probably thinking that it's a performance of some kind, and there in the middle is Bernard, facing off against Scott and Rachael, the couple from the bus that I hadn't seen before.

"Who the hell are they?" I ask Brian and Helen, but they just shrug. It looks like everyone simply assumed that they were friends of someone else.

Bernard is standing on the sand, drawn up to his full four-feet of height, facing Scott and Rachael, who have changed their clothes and look like refugees from a Sisters of Mercy concert, all in black like Matrix fans a decade too early.

Then they draw swords, of all things, and advance on Bernard. Bernard runs and leaps, launching himself at Scott, hitting the tall, thin goth-guy square in the chest and knocking him down. With a speed and ferocity never seen in the whole history of Skegness beach, Bernard fires his fist repeatedly into Scott's face until his hands are red with blood. In a fluid motion he snatches the discarded sword, rolls off the prostrate body and brings the blade down, slicing Scott's head cleanly from his neck.

Everyone goes silent. In the distance, police sirens can be heard approaching, a warning that this is all likely to get even more messy.

"Hand him over, dwarf." The woman says in a deadly serious voice. "You can't hope to win against me." She circles Bernard, waving the tip of her rapier through the air.

"I'm not a dwarf, I'm a midget, bitch! And if you want him, you'll have to go through me." He mirrors her sword motions.

"So be it, midget!" And in a blur, both of them clash swords again and again, every blow instantly countered, the sound of steel hitting and scraping and echoing across the beach. Some of the crowd are actually applauding, somehow imagining that the decapitated figure bleeding on the sand is some sort of special effect.

Bernard leaps twice his own height, jumping over his attacker and lashing out with his sword in mid-arc. As his blade finds its target and bites into her left arm she counters with a thrust and, when Bernard lands badly, we can all tell that something is wrong.

Facing the wrong way, Bernard drops to his knees, his sword falling to the beach as his hands clutch at his side. There's blood seeping though his fingers as Rachael stands behind him, her blade raised high.

"Goodbye, little man. And know that when you are dead, your friend will soon follow you."

Everyone is rooted to the spot, unable to move or even make a sound as her sword sweeps down toward Bernard's neck.

And misses its mark completely.

Bernard falls forward, losing too much blood to move away, but Rachael, her black clothes torn, a slice though her left arm, has fallen too, losing her footing and skidding to the side.

There's a sound, like a low wail on the wind, and she lies on the floor and doubles up. Panting, retching, she feels around for her sword and, finding the hilt stabs at the air above her.

The wail gets worse and blood begins to fall like rain from the air just above Rachael. Her head rises and violently twists through almost a full circle. Over the low sobbing moan the sound of her neck splintering is clearly audible.

And still the blood keeps coming from nowhere.

The police are finally on the scene, predictably just a little too late, and an ambulance pulls up on to the beach and people are herded around, as posts and tape are brought out, the beach fenced off and everyone told to leave the area or risk arrest.

An unmarked black van drives up alongside the ambulance and Bernard, Rachael, Scott and the swords are piled into the back. There's a protest from the ambulance men who are yelling that the midget isn't dead and needs medical help. Identity cards are flashed, the medics are put in their place and the black van speeds off to God knows where.

Slowly, I become aware of Diane clutching my hand so tightly it hurts. Slowly, we all head back to the bus in silence, wondering what our next move should be.

Something happened here today, and sixteen of the twenty people who arrived are heading home with a million questions and no answers.

Nineties

1989 – 1990

And almost overnight, everything changes.

After being a fact of life for almost thirty years and one of the most obvious landmarks of the Cold War, the Berlin Wall is finally pulled down, heralding the beginning of the biggest political climate change since the Second World War. Life in Eastern Europe would never again be the same.

And sure enough, within a couple of months, the biggest MacDonald's outlet in the world is opened in Moscow, the first of its kind to service the people of the Soviet Union. Seven days later the dissolution of the USSR begins and secret talks are held to consider the practicalities of replacing the rouble with the quarter-pounder as the national currency.

As the threat of the Cold War dissipates the rest of the world continues to move into a bold new age. In South Africa, President de Klerk releases Nelson Mandela from prison and begins the end of apartheid segregation. In Germany, the reunification process gets underway and the East conduct their first public elections since 1932. Even Britain and Argentina start talking to each other again, restoring the diplomatic links severed eight years earlier during the Falklands conflict.

Finally, there is a proposition by the British Chancellor of the Exchequer that it might be a really good idea if Europe had a single currency. It would be some years before the Euro would be adopted but eventually trade boundaries and exchange risk would become things of the past and European countries would have a new sense of 'community' and 'fellowship'. Naturally, Britain itself will retain the pound for as long as possible whilst it waits patiently for the invitation to become the fifty-first state of America.

20 June 1990
... I've Toured Around
The World

1990 was the year I first moved to Nottingham from Leicester, leaving behind my dad and my sister, leaving behind the house I grew up in, the house which I had no idea at the time had the body of my mother hidden in the attic.

At almost twenty years of age I would move into a house about four miles from where I live now and take a job as a clerk at an insurance company in town. As a junior member of staff I would earn enough money to pay my rent and spend a modest amount of time drinking with my friends in various pubs around the city centre. Over the next ten years I would meet and marry Samantha Moore, get bogged down with a mundane home life, leave her and slowly start to go off the rails.

Perhaps I should have tried to speak to myself sooner, but the eighties rushed past so quickly that I barely had time to think. Now, on the day the younger me makes the break away from home, everything seems a bit more urgent and, though I have no evidence to back it up, I have a gut feeling that it was this period in my life that I was sent back to sort out.

Diane was now living back with me in the flat and, though I could obviously never tell her about my coming from the future and that my large portfolio of shares was generated by my knowledge of not-yet-developed technology, she was happy to accept that I lived off a large inheritance and a carefully managed investment fund. Indeed, this year my stockholdings climbed again as the Internet finally began to take shape. Over the next few years mankind will have gone from having no global public communications system to compiling the largest pornography database in history. Now *that's* technological growth for you.

Diane moved back in with me about six months ago. Following that weird day at Skegness we'd continued to see each other and had grown closer all the time. Within a couple of months we were inseparable and I began to realise that this was what life was all about. Finally, I was in a truly happy, normal relationship with someone I wasn't actually related to. I had almost no interest at all in sorting out the problems of my younger self. Lurking at the back of my mind was always the worry that if I sorted myself out then maybe I wouldn't be sent back in time in the first place. Always nagging away at me was the worry that sorting out my other self s life would mean that none of this would happen, that I would cease to exist, that the younger me would simply carry on with his life, never knowing what could have been. In short, I had a bad case of a paradox headache.

It was all conjecture of course, but after spending the last twenty years making new mistakes in the past, I wasn't too eager to risk wiping out my whole existence now that I'd finally found real happiness. No, I'd sort out the other Julian if it became absolutely necessary, but otherwise he could just get on with his own life and leave me to finally enjoy mine with Diane.

For a woman who once let a radical lesbian shave all her hair off, Diane was fully committed to making another go of being a hairdresser and I'd used some of my funds to set her up with a small, local shop that kept her busy and turned a nice profit. I also got my own hair cut for free which was an excellent side-effect since I hated going to the barbers and being held captive, forced to talk about where I'm going on holiday or what about that local football team, or how's life at work going? I can just imagine the endless amount of talking that must take place when a taxi driver goes to the barbers. Still, Diane likes it and it makes her happy and she's actually getting a good reputation and a growing line of repeat customers.

So I get to spend my days pottering around, doing the housework, watching daytime television and jotting down ideas for a novel I might write if I can find enough spare time. Every now and then I'm shocked by the realisation that the eighties have gone and it's already the nineties. It seems like only days ago that I was there with Dave, missing my birth as the news of Hendrix's death filtered through the papers. It's twenty years later and by rights I should now be about fifty-six years old. I try not to worry about the fact that I'm not aging. I still look exactly as I did back in 2006, back in 1970, except now I'm growing beard to mask my face and help prevent awkward questions being asked.

Diane was forty this year, though she still looks about a decade younger.

Hopefully in another ten years she'll still be happy and young-looking and won't even stop to question my curious eternal youth.

My not aging is the single thing about my life that makes me think that I only have until 2006 to get things sorted out. In fifteen or sixteen years' time the younger Julian Grant is going to look exactly like I do. What will happen then? If I sort out his problems and clear things up between him and Cassie, maybe as a reward I'll get to carry on with my own life, live things out naturally with Diane. I'm really hoping so since we seem to have developed one of those 'growing old together' kinds of relationships.

Part of me can't help but look at the future as the end of the line, though. In 2006 I'll have reached thirty-six twice over and I'll have gone through over seventy years of mistakes and family relationship crises. That part of me is almost certain that I'll sort out my other life and blink out of existence. I get a cold shiver some nights when I think about it, like being told exactly when you're going to die. I suppose I only have a decade and a half to wait until I finally find out.

The only thing that mars our otherwise happy life together, other than my feeling of impending doom, is that I know Diane still has nightmares about that Pete thing. I can hardly blame her. It wasn't exactly a nice way for him to go. The police were more than satisfied that it was self defence, though explaining to them that I had no idea I was harbouring a known terrorist was a little more difficult. I never told them about Diane. By the time I called in the police she'd packed what few personal possessions she owned and left town. I told them I put Pete up as a favour, that I had my suspicions that he might not be a law-abiding citizen, but I was worried about Pete doing something to me if he found that I'd spoken to the police.

I told them that Pete had gone mental. I told them that he tried to attack me and I only just managed to grab the scissors and it was him or me. I really didn't have a choice.

They accepted the story, seemingly more than happy to have Pete out of the way. One less burden to foist upon the prison system.

They asked about his wife and I told them I didn't even know he was married. He occasionally brought back girls and I generally tried to keep out of his way. I told them about the explosives under the bed and they took away all of Pete's stuff for evidence.

Diane, it seems, had taken any money that might have been lying around.

My life slowly returned to normality and it was two months after the Pete-thing that Diane came back to my flat and asked me to go for a drink with her. She had rented a place in Norfolk under a false name and waited to make sure that the police didn't chase her up. Over a couple of beers she explained that she was getting tired of running away. She'd been out of trouble with the police for almost two years, she needed to stand on her own feet and since I'd pretty much saved her life she figured she'd make her stand in Nottingham, where she hoped that I could keep an eye on her whilst she got her life back on track.

I don't know how much she was attracted to me back then, I don't know if she ever really expected us to get together, and I've definitely never asked her if she occasionally thinks, 'Hang on, this guy looked about thirty-five back in the seventies. What the hell's going on?'

I don't pretend to know what she was thinking, but the rest is, quite literally in my case, history.

The events surrounding that day at Skegness were never fully explained, though after a couple of months in a high security, government hospital, Bernard returned to drinking at the pub, though there was never a second pint on his table and he was much, much quieter than he used to be.

He never spoke about the day on the beach and out of either politeness or awkwardness, no one ever asked him about it either.

It's going to be a different decade now, with different problems to sort through. There's going to have to be a confrontation with my now adult 'other self' at some point, but for now I just have to work on improving the quality of my life with Diane and deal with things the best way I can.

So like I said, I'm growing a beard to make myself look older.

That should deal with everything quite nicely.

1990 – 1991

For a decade that started out with so much promise, things in the nineties declined sharply with the onset of Iraq's invasion of Kuwait. The problems all began when Iraq's leader, a virtually unknown dictator named Saddam Hussein, made claims that Kuwait was drilling into Iraq's oil reserves and therefore he was totally justified in marching on their country and taking a few busloads of hostages.

In what today seems like an old-fashioned way of dealing with things, the United Nations responded by placing trade restrictions on Iraq, asking for the return of any hostages and ordering the complete withdrawal of all troops from Kuwait. Saddam nicely gave up the hostages, but failed to recall his troops and a coalition force was sent in to liberate the Kuwait oil fields.

Of course today it is understood that diplomatic things such as 'trade embargoes' and 'negotiations' are just outmoded ideas with limited success rates. It is equally accepted that UN controlled peace forces are nowhere near as good as hardened squads of US marines led by Chuck Norris and, possibly, David Hasselhoff and that guy out of Air Wolf. It seems that in the twenty-first century all you need to go to war is either 'a good hunch that something is amiss' or an overwhelming urge to clean up a country your dad didn't quite sort out.

But that wasn't the way things were done in the early nineties and the coalition forces won the day and restored peace to the Middle East. Kuwait, with its oil reserves, was forever indebted to the West and America could sleep soundly knowing that the defeated and humiliated country of Iraq would never prove to be a problem ever again.

23 November 1991
... Oh Well, Whatever, Nevermind

Saturday morning, nine o'clock, and I'm standing outside the house I grew up in for the first time in about twelve years. I'm freezing my nuts off and in my near-frostbitten hand is a copy of *The Sun*, its front page emblazoned with rumours that Freddie Mercury from Queen is reported to be suffering from AIDS and doesn't have long to live.

The door I'm looking at is the same peeling green that it was when I was last here and the garden is tidy, but in need of mowing. The windows need a good clean but otherwise the place hasn't changed that much in over a decade. And now I'm actually standing here I can't bring myself to knock on the door. I just stare at the number '15' in brass digits, screwed into the wood at eye-level.

And then the door opens for me anyway and Dave stands there, shorter than I remember, older than he should be.

The last ten years haven't been kind to him and his face looks like it hasn't seen a smile in all that time.

"I saw you walk down the path." He says, matter-of-factly. "You'd better come inside. It's cold and you looked like you might be standing there for some time if I didn't do something about it."

He wanders off into the living room, which has the exact same furniture, same carpets, same wallpaper as it did when I left. I remember the day I first left home, back when I was twenty, how infuriating it was that nothing ever changed, nothing got updated or altered, just left to wear thin and gather dust. It's only now that I realise how closely the house and my father are linked and whilst there's a little more clutter than there used to be this is exactly what Dave wants it to be, a shrine to that single day a dozen years ago.

I'm finding it difficult to come to terms with how much smaller Dave seems to have become, almost as if he's deliberately trying to fade away to nothing. He's standing there as if he hopes to be ignored so much that he ceases to exist and can leave all his troubles behind. The man I used to think of as Dennis Hopper has become more like an aging Clint Eastwood, quiet, drawn and thin, a man who hasn't eaten properly for far too long, like he's forgotten how to do it or more likely just doesn't care.

Looking twenty years older than he actually is, he lowers himself into the same armchair he's always had and makes me realise that the years I spent pining for the woman I lost were nothing to what Dave has clearly been through.

I don't know where to begin and Dave seems content to just sit there, staring into the fireplace until something rouses him. I need to say something so I try to regurgitate the speech I've been working on in my head. It feels like I'm reading him a letter.

"I'm sorry it's been so long, Dave. I needed to get away and I didn't think you'd want me hanging around, making your life difficult." That's right, I'm so selfless. I did it all for him.

"Every passing year made it so much harder to get back in touch with you. I never knew what to say. I never really knew how you felt about things. Eventually, I just gave up trying. I figured you'd be better off without me reminding you of the past."

He coughs out a dry, harsh laugh, devoid of humour, again no trace of anything approaching a smile, but he still doesn't say anything. I hold out the paper I've been carrying.

"I see the pop stars keep dying. Do you ever see anything of the old Hendrix gang? I ran into Pete and Diane a couple of years back." It's like trying to talk to someone in a mental hospital. Half the time I'm not even sure that he hears me. I decide not to tell him that Diane and I are getting married next year. "Ever see anything of Steve? I heard on the grapevine that he was thinking of moving to Hollywood to pitch his idea for a sequel to *Gone with the Wind*. I think it had robots in it."

Dave shakes his head. "I keep myself to myself these days. Marie is about the only person who comes to visit me, her and that imbecile of a husband she insisted on marrying. She's pregnant, you know, turning me into a grandfather."

He's just making small talk, skirting around anything of importance. I try to push ahead with some light banter.

"I hear that Jim Morrison is back from the dead and trying to regain his rightful place as heir to the supermarket empire. They say it'll be tied up in the courts for years." And I'm beginning to think I shouldn't have come back, wondering how long I can hold out before I make my excuses and head back home.

"The conspiracies and the past are dead now, Julian. Like so much of me. It feels like most of my life died when Jenny left me."

Left him. Have things got so bad now that Dave believes his own lies? Has he been sitting here amongst the relics of the past so long that he actually thinks she's run away with someone to Croydon?

"I didn't like to ask. You don't look so well, Dave."

"I've suffered a bit, nothing I can't deal with, but my health isn't what it used to be."

"You'll do fine." And for once I can tell him something that isn't a lie.

I know that his health isn't great, but he does at least make it to the next century.

"No doubt. So why come back now? After all this time? Worried I'd go crazy and tell people how you hid my wife in the attic?"

It takes a minute for the numb, icy feeling to leave my spine.

I don't suppose I should be that surprised that he found her. It's quite a hefty amount of wishful thinking to expect someone to never question the new sealed cabinet that's mysteriously appeared in their loft. "No. I just... I just wanted to see you again. It's been so long, and I left with so much hanging in the air."

I came back for absolution. I came back to hear you tell me that you don't blame me for Jenny's death. After all this time I still need to hear someone tell me that it wasn't my fault.

He gets up and walks through to the kitchen. "Do you want a drink?"

"Just a glass of water, please."

I look around the living room for the single framed photo of Dave, Jenny, Marie and my other self on holiday in Whitby. I stand at the mantelpiece and pick it up, remembering how I used to look at this photo every day as a teenager, this dusty echo of a mother I never really knew. By the time I left home I'd spent over ten years making up an idea of a mother based on this one picture. In my head I'd managed to construct the perfect, always smiling, happy family that should never have broken up.

Dave comes back and hands me a glass. He sits down again with an old, cracked silver jubilee mug filled with coffee. Not for the first time in my life it feels like I've stepped back in time. I hold up the photo.

"You know, I don't actually have any pictures of her? Nothing to remember her by. I knew her for almost ten years and then nothing, like she was never even here."

Except for the nightmares.

"Oh, she was here." He slurps at his coffee. "I first met her at school, you know. We shared a class when we were about nine years old. She'd only recently moved to the area and I showed her around, told her the people to watch out for, the teachers you shouldn't upset. We were childhood sweethearts and back then I still had those childish thoughts of us growing old together, but obviously-"

He cuts off from a line of thought he doesn't want to tread, a future now hopelessly out of reach.

"I waited for the police to come for me for years and still do, truth be told. I was sure that Mrs Kennedy next door would have said something, reported me or at least claimed that there had been some sort of disturbance. But if anything, she took me under her wing. She used to make me cottage pies from time to time, she used to say that she knows how difficult it is bringing up kids on your own and wanted me to know that she was always there if I needed someone to talk to."

I remembered those pies. They weren't too bad either. "Sounds like you had an admirer."

"No. Well, at least not as far as I was concerned. Jenny will always be the only woman for me, even now she's gone. Anyway, Mrs Kennedy moved away about five years ago. I miss the pies, but not the five screaming kids running around all the time."

"I didn't want you to find her. I hoped she'd just stay hidden. Leave no-one any the wiser."

"Three years after you left, Marie and Julian went up there playing house games or something, they tidied everything up and when I went up there to check on them I noticed the box at the end. I knew I hadn't put it there, it was fairly new and I hadn't been in the roof for years. It didn't take a genius to work out where you had hidden her.

"Once I knew, well, it made sleeping in the house fairly difficult so I sent the kids to my mother's for a weekend and brought her back down. I never opened the case but I knew it was her. There were points where I didn't think I could go through with it, but I managed to bury her in the back garden, planted a new flower bed for her. It's more fitting, I think. I just have to stay here until I die to make sure she never gets found."

He makes it all sound so mundane. Like burying a body in your back garden is just one of those things you have to do from time to time, like the weeding.

"I'm really sorry, Dave." I just don't know what else I can say to him.

"Don't be. I've had long enough to come to terms with what I did. I still have trouble sleeping some nights but I know I can't bring her back. I brought up the kids as best I could and you got me out of a nasty situation. Sometimes I wonder if I should go to the police, but what good would that really do?"

And this is where everything has brought me, to a covered up accidental death, to a man diminished by his own failings, to a man robbed of his future because of me and my cheating. How many lives have been messed up because of my lies and infidelities?

"How are Marie and Julian?"

"Like I say, Marie has got herself pregnant at eighteen, already married to some waster and is probably going to throwaway a perfectly good career in favour of raising a family. Julian has moved to Nottingham. He couldn't stand to be around his tired, old father any longer. I thought about replacing both of them with a dog. I might still do it, if only for the company."

He motions for me to pass him the photo, the four faces from the past, happily smiling at the camera back in 1977. I remember when it was taken during a visit to a Zoo. The day had ended with me having a tantrum because I couldn't take one of the monkeys home with me and mum lost her temper while Marie kept asking over and over again why one of the zebras was trying to get a piggy-back from another zebra. It seemed like chaos, but at least we were still a family. I wonder now how much of that memory is made up, like so much of my past seems to have been.

Dave looks at the photo longingly, at the lost family he can never get back. "The funny thing is, and other people who were around back then have remarked on it too, that as Julian grew up and filled out he started to look quite a lot like you."

I laugh as nervously as I can and make some excuse like it's the way that owners start looking like their pets, that I must have been a defining influence on my little name-sake.

But it's total crap and Dave knows this as much as I do. I know where's he's heading and don't really have time to stop him jumping to the wrong conclusion.

"I was angry for a long time, Julian." He says, putting the photo back down on the coffee table. "I felt that everyone around me was laughing behind my back. You turned up out of the blue, you pretended to be a family friend and you even got Jenny to name the kid Julian. Like it was all just some sick joke. I spent a lot of time wondering if I should track you down, find you and hurt you like you'd hurt me.

"I could have at least made you answer my questions. How long had you known her? Did she love you more than me? Was Marie your child, too? You'd messed up and got her pregnant with your child and managed to insinuate yourself back into her life so you could watch as someone else brought up your child. You get all the fun and good old Dave gets all the screaming and dirty nappies. And then, when the stress and strain of bringing up a kid has driven a wedge between me and Jenny, you'd be there to step in and fill the breach."

He's still not actually angry. The anger has come and gone, he's just recounting the facts, telling me a story that he's too tired and old to worry about any more. I can't tell him anything that would make sense to him so I just let him continue, see where he goes, and when he finishes, he'll probably hit me and I'll walk away feeling that somehow justice has been served.

"Do you know how embarrassing it is to know that people are talking behind your back? Stupid old Dave lets his supposedly best mate shag his own girlfriend and then brings up his kid. They all thought it. My friends and family all think it was you that she ran away with."

"Dave, it's not like that." I begin, but where can I go with this? He's got it wrong, but the truth is ridiculous. He's got some of the facts wrong, but I was seeing his wife behind his back for years. He knows full well that the night she died was as much down to me as it was to him.

"I ignored the comments and the looks, and I brought Julian up as if he was mine. I did the best I could for him and Marie and I let everything else slide. If I ever saw you again, and there'd be no reason I should, I'd probably just ignore you. Having your confession wouldn't make an ounce difference, it wouldn't bring her back. Having you admit the truth could only resurrect the pain.

"And yet here you are. Back at the scene of the crime. Back to rub salt in my wounds. Or that's what I thought when I first saw you walk down my path. But I'm wrong aren't I?" He stares me straight in the eyes. "Tell me, Julian, what really brought you back?"

I don't know what to tell him. I find that I'm close to tears myself, emotions welling up that I thought I'd covered over and hidden from sight. I pick up the photo and a tear falls onto the glass. "I miss her so much," is all I can say.

And Dave is suddenly standing beside me, his arm round my shoulders, looking more certain and whole than he's been in years and, so very quietly, he says, "She was the mother you never knew."

And my tears flood out as he holds on to me and stops me falling to the floor.

My father watches in silence as I sit on the sofa staring intently at a patch of carpet near the tiled fireplace. Ten, fifteen minutes pass before I finally find my voice again. I don't know what to say, I've never known what to say. "I never knew how to tell you."

"I probably wouldn't have believed you if you tried. I watched you this morning when you came through the gate. I was looking out of the window like I always expected you to be coming and when I saw you there, even with that beard, it was all just so obvious. You can't hide the truth from your own father. Not forever anyway." He slowly asks, "Did Jenny know?"

"No. I don't think so."

"I don't suppose you can tell me how you did it? How you came back?"

Now I'm laughing. "I don't have a clue! I'm here and as far as I can tell I'm waiting for something. In a few years your son is going to get in trouble and I think I've been sent here to sort it out. It makes no sense to me. After all these years I still can't even try to explain it."

I realise now why this trip was necessary, that I've managed to lift a weight from my father's shoulders, even though I can never tell him the whole truth. He thinks he has answers and for the first time in years he believes that his wife didn't cheat on him. Not with me anyway. I can let him think that, give him back some degree of happiness, and now he has his best friend back, and more than that, his son, who left and never gets in touch, has returned too. I still know that I've cheated him, but now that secret is mine alone.

"I suppose you have all sorts of stuff you can't tell me about the future? Can't risk changing the course of history and all that?"

"I know some things, and to be honest I'm not sure if the future can be changed or not. But I know you survive and if it helps you sleep better, the police don't arrest you and Marie turns out to be a lawyer. Still married to that Kevin bloke, though, I'm afraid."

"How far ahead do you know things?"

"2006. It's a scary place where everyone has a flying car like in Back to the Future and there's a war brewing between the humans and their android slaves, but apart from that, things aren't so different."

I don't know how much I should tell him and I don't know how much he wants to know. But this journey here today has opened some doors I thought were locked and barred forever.

And there's still one more thing I need to do.

"I think I should go outside and say goodbye to her properly."

1991 – 1992

In religious news, Pope John Paul II finally admits that the trial of Galileo Galilei, some three hundred and thirty years earlier, may have been mishandled by the Catholic Church. In light of certain pieces of new evidence collected by the space shuttle and other science boffins, it appears that Galileo may have been correct in his assumption that the Earth revolves around the Sun and not the other way round. The Church would like to point out that although Galileo may have been right in this one case, the following Catholic tenets still stand:

The Earth was definitely created in just six days.

Evolution is clearly a bunch of nonsense with no facts to back it up.

You cannot see God, touch God, Speak to God, hear God, or, should you desire to, taste God. He is invisible to all five senses and hasn't actually spoken to anyone for thousands of years. He nonetheless exists and anyone who says otherwise is a heretic.

The problems faced in the whole science versus religion argument pales into insignificance, however, when compared to the problems I had thanks to a typing error I found in a school RE textbook when I was eleven years old. I was informed that the Devil, or Santa, lives in Hell and tortures people who have lived bad lives.

For years I spent every Christmas Eve hiding under my bed, waiting for some red demon to come down the chimney and hoping that this year I wasn't on Santa's 'Naughty' list.

Galileo got off relatively easily.

25 April 1992
... Sometimes I Feel Like I Don't Have a Partner

We decided that we didn't want the whole big wedding ceremony with all the trimmings. I'd been married before, in about two years time, and Diane had barely seen her family in twenty years and didn't really have any great urges to rekindle old relationships. Add to that the logistics of pulling together dysfunctional family members from around the country and paying for them all to get pissed and you've got more of a headache than either of us wanted to go through.

So we opted for a quiet registry office affair and a trip away to somewhere warm with enough cash to not have to worry about how much anything cost. By the time it's dark we're sitting in a restaurant in Venice ordering pasta and wine and commenting time and again on what a good idea it was to ignore the family for once.

After dinner and dessert we walked around Venice, taking in the strangely green water of the canals and the sometimes breathtaking, other times crumbling architecture, before heading back to the hotel. In the silence of the narrow streets I joked a couple of times about how much it was like the film *Don't Look Now* where Donald Sutherland works in Venice and gets murdered by a midget-woman in a red coat.

And then it's all funky music, disco lights, breasts and naked flesh as the wedding night duties are performed and we both fall asleep hot, sweaty and panting.

Next thing, the luminous dial of the travel clock on the bedside table says it's around 3.00am and I'm woken by the sound of something outside the hotel window. Something outside is scratching at the glass.

And although I don't want to, I get out of bed and stand beside the curtain listening, not wanting to draw them open. I imagine birds, maybe a cat, scratching away, possibly a late night window cleaner or an emergency repairman. I try not to imagine the ugly midget in the red coat getting ready to leap in and stab me. I try not to think about the vampire children from *Salem's Lot* beckoning me to join them.

Every ten seconds or so there's a scrape, scrape sound, like a rat. I've never heard that Venice has a particular rat problem, although there's quite a lot in the third Indiana Jones film, though they were in the sewers and not scratching at the fourth floor window of a hotel. But maybe that's it. Rats. No need to worry, no need to look. Just get back into bed, where Diane is sleeping peacefully, unaware that an army of unknown horrors is lurking on the other side of the curtains.

So I'm back in the nice soft bed, where I can lie down and stare into the dark, listening to the scraping noise for another five minutes. This is a truly wonderful start to my honeymoon and I'll be lucky if I'm fit for anything in the morning. I'll be lucky if I ever get back to sleep.

Another five minutes pass and once, for almost a whole two minutes, the scratching noise stops. I'm not sure if the silence is worse than the scratching, but it's back soon enough and I know that eventually I will have to open the curtains and shoo away whatever animal is trying to get into my room.

Or a midget in a red coat. Ugly as sin.

With a knife.

I'm beginning to wish I never watched any films.

I momentarily toy with the idea of waking up Diane, but there's not a lot of point disturbing her and scaring her witless, although part of me wishes that I could just rouse her and she'd tell me I'm imagining things and I should just go back to sleep.

Once again I'm out of bed, stepping across the carpet on tiptoe, avoiding the clothes strewn here and there, heading for the curtains. I have to open them, just to check for certain that nothing's there, then I can go back to sleep.

It's probably just a tree hitting the window or something.

Once, one winter when I lived in Leicester, I was woken at around five in the morning, scared stiff because something was scraping at my house door. It was the same sort of noise, scrape, scrape, scrape, over and over, but this only went on for a couple of minutes and turned out to be someone scraping ice off their car windscreen.

In Venice, in the springtime, there was unlikely to be someone scraping ice off their car outside a fourth floor hotel window.

More the sort of place you'd find a midget in a red coat.

The scraping has stopped. Nothing now for maybe three minutes. I put an index finger between the curtains and make the smallest chink to look through, expecting to see the face of some deformed dwarf looking back at me. But there's nothing there.

I open them up and unlock the French window that leads to the balcony, and it's dark and there doesn't appear to be anyone out there waiting to slice me apart. I open the doors and step through, the warm night air hitting my skin.

Nothing. Just Venice, dark and silent around me.

I kneel down and look at the window frame, inspecting the paintwork near the floor. It's old and peeling, but there's no sign that something has just spent fifteen minutes trying to break in.

Then something falls from the building, a plant pot or some masonry hitting the floor nearby. Standing, I look over the balcony but can't see anything in the street below. For a moment all I hear is the gentle lapping sound of the water in the canal, disturbed by a solitary boat slowly making its way through the night.

Then I hear the footsteps, running, echoing.

I'm almost certain that I only imagine the flash of a red coat.

A cool breeze seems to pick up and rush past me into the room and as it breathes past my ears I'm sure I hear a voice whispering, "It's all over." I back into the hotel room and lock the window shut. I close the curtains and retreat to the bed, silently praying that the scratching won't start up again. Beside me, Diane is still sleeping soundly.

It's maybe an hour later when I finally manage to join her.

1992 – 1993

A new theme park is set to open later this year on a small island somewhere near Costa Rica where, for the right price, parents and children alike can go on a wild safari ride through the jungle checking out the wildlife in its natural habitat.

The difference here is that this theme park doesn't show you common or garden lions, tigers and giraffes. This park purports to contain actual living dinosaurs.

The island has been named 'Jurassic Park' and is the brain child of eccentric billionaire, John Hammond. Hammond has funded years of research into controversial cloning techniques and now claims to be able to give the public a real taste of pre-history.

"We have everything from a Dilophosaurus to a Tyrannosaurus rex," declares Hammond. "When I was a child I always used to love watching films and reading books with dinosaurs in them. Now I get to keep them as pets! "

And whilst we might think that domestic pets like Tiddles and Fido can be a bit of a handful around the house, Mr Hammond says that his 'pets' are completely under control and there is absolutely no danger of them escaping and attacking the park's visitors.

"No, no, no!" He exclaims. "At Jurassic Park we have consumer safety as our absolute top priority! And besides, you're forgetting our motto, 'If it doesn't eat you, it can only make you stronger'. Just my little joke. I assure you, no one has ever been eaten here. Not even a little bit."

Tickets for holidays at the park go on sale next month and cost a small fortune, so get saving up now.

23 June 1993
... I Cry Sometimes When I'm Lying in Bed

The remainder of the honeymoon was scratch-free and, although my sleep was a little disturbed by images of hordes of insane, ugly dwarves chasing me through the canals with knives, no actual little people turned up to bother me. I didn't mention it to Diane, who was doing a first-rate job of keeping me otherwise occupied with a honeymoon full of unparalleled, feverish sex. I put the whole thing down to an overexcited mouse or a bird and left it at that. I also cut back on my late night cheese intake for good measure.

When we got back to Nottingham and settled down, Diane threw herself into cutting people's hair whilst I went about setting up several companies designed to take advantage of the recently established 'World Wide Web'.

Still an incredible thing that amazed the general public, this 'internet' was a means to circulate whole databases full of information effortlessly and almost free of charge around the world using computers. And whilst many people were in awe of this technological masterpiece, many other people at the time suspected that we were nearing the sci-fi world of Terminator and that within a few short years the machines would rise up to take their place as the natural rulers of mankind. In the press only a month ago a research team from Cambridge had postulated that if technology continued to progress at its current rate, there would be a computer-brain ruling the Earth by the year 1999. There was even a rumour that some sort of 'bug' would infect all computers at midnight on the eve of the year 2000. This bug, scientists hypothesised, would prevent man from controlling his machines and trigger the third world war, finally demoting mankind to an almost extinct slave-class ruled over by computer controlled apes. Even members of the more reputable churches were dubbing the internet 'the communications system of Satan' and claiming that to really ensure you gained access to heaven you needed to give up all your worldly possessions and live in a commune in Texas.

Personally, I just set up about twenty companies delivering pornography to the masses, which were totally supported by advertising revenue. I left the actual running of the companies to various managers and just kept an occasional eye on the overall state of play. Within a couple of years I'll have people ordering perfectly legal mail order brides whilst at the same time taking advantage of certain loopholes in international law that will let me trade in human organs.

It doesn't take Einstein to see that the world at the birth of the internet is a very special, under-policed, place, desperate to be taken advantage of by someone with scruples like mine.

By this time I was also developing a tricky network of companies through which to divest my earnings without anyone finding out exactly who was running things. I may not be able to affect history, but I can, it seems, amass huge sums of money now that the long-awaited computer revolution is finally underway.

Due to the complexity of the companies I've set up, I have to head down to London every now and then to speak with my so-called 'financial advisors', who seem to think that the amount of money I've invested in the internet is a mistake. They told me to put my money somewhere safe and steady like construction companies, medicines and insurance. They think I'm mad, but the dot-corn boom is just around the corner and this time I certainly won't be missing out on my share of the hefty financial rewards available to the wily investor.

In just a few short years the whole world will be connected to the web and I'll be getting a slice of every pound, dollar or yen they spend. My economic future is finally rosy beyond belief and all I have to do is stay clear of the no-no's like hard drugs and children and the hunger of the repressed world for difficult-to-find filth will make me a rich man.

If you get your jollies from bondage, but don't like to collect your copy of *Lubed up in Latex* from the old woman at the newsagents, then the internet is for you.

Like to see animals in various states of undress, but find it difficult to ask Mr Patel to order you *Kinky Chimps Tea Party*? Just log on and within seconds you'll be happily spanking the monkey till the cows come home.

And every click, every link, and every sponsored banner will bring me advertising revenue and wads of cash. Alright, at present the world is stuck with pretty basic computers and broadband is a few years off, but the secret to my success is all in the planning. My advisors are naturally cautious, but me, with my 2003 pound coin and a basic knowledge of the future, I'm in a prime position to finally take over the world.

Okay, perhaps not quite the world, but I'll certainly be rich enough to afford anything I want, and I might even use some of the cash to improve humanity or help widows and orphans or something.

Today is also the day we move into our new house. A detached, four bedroom place in a small village just outside of Nottingham. The flat has served us well, but since Diane moved in it's become a bit cramped and there's still the memory of Pete spurting blood all over the carpet to contend with. Better all round to get a place of our own and for a nice reasonable price too, since the housing boom isn't scheduled until the start of the next century.

It's the start of a new life for me and I finally feel that I'm settled in for good here in the past and that with Diane at my side things can only get even better. We're financially and romantically secure, we're happy and we're in love. And who knows, maybe someday there will be the pitter-patter of little feet to keep us company.

In today's news I'm intrigued to see that story about the Bobbitt guy whose wife cut off his penis and threw it out of her car window. I remember how famous he became and how the police managed to find his discarded manhood and got it reattached. I also remember that his wife got off by pleading insanity. She claimed in her defence that her husband didn't give her any orgasms so she cut off his cock. Perfectly sound American behaviour that.

And someday in the not too distant future, John Wayne Bobbitt will go on to appear in the high quality porn film, *Frankenpenis*, which will be available to buy online through one of my websites and returns us once again to the revenue-making, marketing power of my new saviour, the internet.

1993 – 1994

The United States television-viewing public is treated to the first episode of a comedy series entitled simply, *Friends*, little knowing that this was just the tip of the iceberg for a programme that was eventually destined to run for more than two hundred and thirty episodes.

The series set out to follow the exploits of six buddies as they move from being twenty-somethings to thirty-somethings in New York, though, by the time the series finally came to an end, a couple of them had actually managed to make the leap to being forty-somethings,.

Being friends, the characters did all the things friends normally do, like borrowing money, eating everyone's food, sleeping with each other and having bizarre drug-induced, flashback episodes in order to keep the budgets down and leave enough cash for high quality guest stars like the Duchess of York and Magnum PI.

Elsewhere around the world, crowds were flocking to see the new US President Bill Clinton in his '*Sticking my Nose In*' World Tour '94. Bill was heading off around the globe, making a name for himself, getting into photo opportunities with famous world leaders and generally trying to look like he was solving conflicts wherever he touched down.

And Anglo-French relationships are strengthened when, after years of development and construction, the Channel Tunnel finally opens, linking the two countries for the first time since the last ice age and providing illegal immigrants and asylum seekers with far better access to the United Kingdom than they had ever been granted in the past.

23 September 1994
... Sometimes My Mind Plays Tricks on Me

One of the biggest mistakes of my old life was getting married when I did.

Too young and too quick with our relationship not as sound as we both thought it was. There could be a million reasons that the marriage didn't work out, but when it broke down we both blamed each other, we couldn't see any point of view but our own and we each went our separate ways knowing there was nothing left to fight for. Released from the marriage, I tried to make up for lost time. I always felt I hadn't fully explored my sexuality before I settled down, that I needed time to get out there, look around a bit and try new and different things.

When I look back now, some of those things were mistakes. In fact, most of those things were mistakes. One bad idea followed one bad relationship time and time again.

Of course, when I first met Samantha Moore we got along like we'd known each other forever, like we had always been lifelong friends. That first few months of happiness when it seems like you've met the most perfect person in the world, when you feel strong enough as a couple to take on anything that might get thrown at you. The sort of feeling that fades after six months, just one month after you've gone and got married in a hasty ceremony that should, in retrospect, have been postponed a while.

The marriage lasted a little under a year. I didn't really know anything about settling down and looking out for someone else, and she wasn't much better. We argued and we sniped whenever the opportunity arose and we accused each other of every sort of infidelity. Ultimately, no one had actually cheated on anyone, we just realised that the whole 'being together' thing was simply wrong. One final argument on a cold day next winter and I, the other me, will never see Sam again. I look back at that day, for me almost thirty-five years ago, and it all seems so pointless. I can see now that we should have tried harder, should have made an effort. Then again, perhaps we should never have teamed up together in the first place. One day everything seems fine and we're superficially playing happy families where I'm the dutiful son-in-law spending Christmas with her and her parents, she spends New Year with me, my father and Marie. Then she's suddenly gone, out of my life like she never even existed.

She broke my heart back then. I half-heartedly argued that we should try harder and give it another go. She just didn't see the point. I don't know if my life would have been better if she'd stayed. Maybe my younger self would have been better off if Samantha Moore had never entered our life. It's enough of a 'maybe' to finally get me to intervene in my previous life.

23 September 1994 was still, after all these years, etched into my memory. A Friday night, me out in town patrolling the bars with my mates from work, looking for girls to cop off with and maybe take back to the house I shared with three other guys. Usually, these sort of nights ended in a takeaway pizza and possibly, in wasn't too drunk, a wank over the ten free minutes of late night soft-porn we got through the satellite system. Very occasionally these nights would end up with me taking a girl back to the house, attempting to fight through the beer and get a half usable hard-on, fumbling with her for ten minutes or so before passing out and waking up the next day with a hangover and someone who wasn't quite the beautiful supermodel I remembered from the drunken haze and flashing lights of the night club.

But 23 September 1994 was different. It was the night I met Sam.

Memory is an incredible thing. So many times I've been amazed by television programmes I saw as a child, that were particularly important or funny, when they come out on video or DVD, bear only a passing resemblance to what I thought I'd seen. Scenes I knew so well would have totally different dialogue, people would be wearing different clothes or things would be a totally different colour. So many times the video evidence has proved me wrong. And if that's the case with TV and films, where the reality of events can be proved, how much more at fault is my memory of everyday life where no proof exists?

Back in 1975 I was bought a huge, orange Space-Hopper with a big grinning face on it, only to find that, when 1975 came round again and I was there as a grown man, that it was a fairly small, green Space-Hopper with a big grinning face. I'd just upgraded the memory of a well loved childhood toy with the bog-standard colour and size I thought Space-Hoppers should be.

How many more things just like that have I managed to misremember? How many of my relationship problems with Sam have I attributed to her when they were actually down to me? Is my memory of the whole relationship a lie? Well, I figure that the easiest way to sort out all the problems is to make sure that my other self and her never get to meet. This time, the future is getting changed and I'm going to save myself a lot of pain, hurt and grief by changing it.

Tonight, at 8.30pm I would be in *Yates'*, standing at the interior balcony, looking down on the crowd below as more and more people came out drinking. It was a standard opening to a night out, standing up there, trying desperately to catch sight of an extra-large cleavage, watching people dancing and bouncing around in the hope that someone would accidentally pop out.

I've held off meeting myself for so long now that I'm starting to wonder again if it's a particularly good idea. Over the last three years I've managed to spy on the younger Julian a couple of times, hanging around his street or near the office he still works at. I've never had the balls to make that final push and actually talk to him. I've never actually let him see me, come to that.

It's now just after eight o'clock and I've been in the pub since seven.

I've tried to slow down my drinking to prevent me getting pissed as a fart, but it's not really helping. From memory I can recall the general way this night unfolds, burned into my head as it is.

At around nine o'clock me and my mates will move on from here to *Bolero*, some sort of tribute bar to the ice skaters, Torville and Dean, where they serve cheap drinks until ten and the bouncers are not too picky about asking the girls for proof of age. In that bar we run into a group of girls out for a hen night, one of whom is Sam, a beauty therapist from Kent, back up here to renew old acquaintances and to attend the wedding of a friend from school. As the girls and blokes pair off, Samantha will take pity on the awkward young Julian Grant who's left alone and dance with him. The dance leads to kissing, the kissing to fondling, the fondling to another round of drinks and from there it's a taxi back home and, after convincing Samantha to move up to Nottingham, they'll get married.

There was probably some sex in the middle of all that, but as I say, memory can be a bit hazy at times.

So my idea is simple. Stop Julian from going to *Bolero* and you stop him messing up his life with an untidy marriage and maybe, by the time Cassie comes along in 2002 he'll be mature enough not to screw up his relationship with her too.

At quarter-past eight I catch sight of myself, standing, holding a pint and staring like a sex-starved idiot at the women on the floor below. There are a lot of older men surrounding him doing exactly the same thing, and not for the first time I'm more than happy to be walking around in the body of a thirty-six year old.

The twenty-four year old Julian is thinner than me. He hasn't spent the last fifteen years cramming beer and pizza down his throat. He looks awkward, his dress sense could be better and he needs the correcting influence of a good steady girlfriend. At the minute he's wearing a white shirt and black trousers. Nothing too extravagant, though I seem to remember that I used to wear some horrendous, multicoloured shirts and had little real idea at all about what actually looked good on a night out.

Perhaps I'm wrong to try and avert his impending marriage. Maybe he needs Sam more than I remember. Then again, there'll be other girls, maybe better girls. Best to stick to the original plan and do my best to change the future.

One of his mates, a university student called John who, if memory serves me right, throws himself in front of a train over some bad exam results next year, has noticed me staring and points me out to Julian and before I know it our eyes meet for the first time since he was nine years old.

I break eye-contact and wander further away, forcing myself to look over the balcony and pick out random details below. What the hell do I tell him? If I try and get him to stay with me for the evening he'll probably think I'm trying to come on to him. I could follow them to *Bolero*, but then I'd risk running into Sam and that might be even more awkward.

"You got a problem?"

I know the voice. It's the voice of myself heard on a tape recording, the way I sound to the outside world, the voice that to me sounds, well, a bit gay. I probably sound the same even now. Hopefully both of us have had enough to drink that he won't notice.

I look at him, feigning surprise, hoping my longer hair will hide my eyes, that my beard will make my face seem different, that the extra years and weight I carry compared to him will make me unrecognisable.

"Sorry?" I say.

"You were staring at me. Over there. I didn't like it." I don't - remember being so confrontational toward people as a younger man. Time changes everyone, I suppose and I'm suddenly becoming aware that I may not even like this version of me from the nineties.

"I didn't mean to. You reminded me of someone."

"I don't think so."

I might as well go for it. "You look like someone I used to know. A kid named Julian Grant. He used to live in Leicester."

He just stares at me and the music seems to get louder as the DJ starts playing '*All That She Wants*' by Ace of Base.

"That's you isn't it?" I ask. "Jenny and Dave's kid? I used to be a friend of your parents back in the seventies. I used to look after you sometimes when they went out."

Recognition slowly dawns, thankfully only recognising me as someone he knew from his childhood. "Oh. The other Julian." I'm not sure what's going through his head right now, for someone I should know intimately this is more like talking to a total stranger.

"Julian Grey." I say to him, forcing him along. "I was sorry to hear about your parents splitting up."

"Yeah? Rumour has it that she went off with you."

That memory thing again. I can't even be sure now what things I remember from when I was in my twenties. Only now, talking with myself, do I start to recall the bitterness I used to feel, the stories that went around during my teenage years, the hushed conversations between my father and my grandparents hinting that they thought my mother had run away with some friend of the family. I remember wondering what it would be like to meet the man who stole my mother away from me. I always had this childish notion that one day I'd find her again. Only now, staring at myself, seeing the hate building up inside him, do I fully remember how much I truly suffered from the loss of my mother.

"She didn't leave your father for me. I was as surprised as anyone when I heard she'd vanished."

I can tell he doesn't believe me.

His mates are heading over, wanting to move on. I don't have the time to develop a rapport here. Trying to talk to him in the pub, around his friends and through the music, was a mistake. I should have visited him earlier.

Irrational thoughts go through my mind that I could have drugged him, kidnapped him, anything to try and make the future change, to stop him meeting Samantha Moore. To stop him making this one, massive mistake.

But they're here, and John, taller than me, looks me in the eye and tries to assert his presence, tries to intimidate me by standing between me and Julian, "Ready to go, Jay?"

He finishes off his pint and drops his glass down on a table. "Sure. We're finished."

"Julian?" I ask as he turns his back on me. "Can I meet up with you sometime? Catch up on things?"

"I don't think so." His contempt for me is totally unexpected, yet now completely understood. I know in my heart that nothing will make my younger self trust me.

"Good luck with those exams, John." I say under my breath as I watch them wander off down the stairs.

I have another drink and give them half an hour before heading off to *Bolero* and making my way toward anything that looks like it might be a hen party. I'm getting pretty drunk now and the only thing left for me to do is divert Samantha's attention before she sympathy-fucks my younger self and damns us both.

And when I locate the girls and actually see Samantha after all this time, I realize that there's just no way I can go through with this. She's gorgeous, she's pretty and she's funny. She's exactly like I remember her from that first night, months before things started to go sour. She smiles in the exact same way that Diane does when she looks at me.

I had the insane thought that I could maybe pull Sam and get her out of the bar before Julian arrived. I could take her to a hotel and save my future. If I could just stop Julian and her meeting on this one night it would be a good enough reason to cheat on Diane.

But I can't. It isn't.

And I realize that, as much as I need Diane in my life, my younger self needs Samantha Moore and Samantha Moore needs him. Once again the future turns out to be set in stone and the joke is on me.

And I watch from a dark corner of the pub as their eyes meet and his future is sealed. Then I leave and go home to sleep with my wife.

1994 – 1995

Trial by Television begins in the United States as former 'football' star OJ Simpson is put in the dock to fight against claims that he murdered his ex-wife and her new lover in Los Angeles.

Simpson was listed as the prime suspect in the case and, rather than give himself up as he had promised, OJ grabbed himself some cash, a gun and a fake beard and engaged police and reporters in a low speed chase through the highways of California. An estimated 95 million Americans tuned in to watch at least part of the pursuit, achieving better viewing figures than anything else in TV history except the last episode of *M*A*S*H*.

With TV bosses convinced that they had a hit on their hands, the trial displaced many soaps and became a daytime hit for months. Special guests were lined up and calls went out to the agents who dealt with Ironside and Quincy, hoping that they would join in the proceedings by becoming expert witnesses.

Finally, during the closing months of the trial, the defence called in OJ's adoptive parents, Homer and Marge Simpson, and his long time friends Barney Gumble and Moe Szyslak. In a defining moment of the case, these witnesses were thrown out of the courtroom and were not allowed to give evidence on the grounds that they were all clearly fictitious. This argument apparently didn't apply to the evidence for the prosecution and the whole escapade caused enough doubt to allow the jury to return a verdict of not guilty.

OJ later went on to appear in the less popular *OJ2: The Civil Case*, but the public had pretty much lost interest and had gone back to watching repeats of Santa Barbara.

24 August 1995
... She Totally Confused all the Passing Piranhas

The clock tells me it's the early hours of the morning when I wake up and find that Diane is nowhere to be seen. The room is dark and the bed beside me is cold. She's probably been gone for some time. It's another warm, end of summer night and the window is open for some fresh air, the curtains dancing a little in the glow from an overly bright moon.

I hit the switch on the bedside lamp and wipe the sleep from my eyes, and I'm wondering where she is when I start to hear that soft, scratching sound again.

Somewhere, possibly from the wall, maybe from the wardrobe, something is scratching and scraping. It's the same noise I heard in Venice, just about the same time on the clock, the same intermittent pauses as if the thing is trying deliberately to get my attention, estimating the point at which I'm most on edge before it starts scraping again.

It waits, as if it knows that my first feeling is relief, but also that I expect it to continue. It waits, and waits, just a little longer than before, just enough to make me think it's finally stopped, before beginning anew.

My mind flashes back to Venice, to the footsteps, to the copy of *Don't Look Now*, which I had in my collection of DVDs in 2006.

Scrape, scrape, pause. Scrape, pause.

It, whatever it is, is definitely in the wardrobe. It must have got in through the open window and found its way in there.

There's panic rising inside my chest and I keep thinking, *where the hell is Diane? What has it done with Diane?* And I leap from the bed, pull open the wardrobe door and something black and leathery flies into my face and disappears into the shadows of the room.

I'm on my knees, panicking and, unable to see where the bat, or whatever it was, went, I notice that inside the wardrobe there are cuttings of newspapers, littering the floor, taped to the backboard and even coming out of the pockets of the shirts hanging there.

'Death of a Princess' says one. Another, *'Gulf War II'*

A third has something about Afghanistan but before I can focus properly there's a fluttering behind me and the bedside lamp crashes to the floor, the bulb exploding on impact.

There's no way there can be newspapers here from the future. There is no way any of this is happening. It's all a dream. All I need to do is wake up.

But I'm too scared to open my eyes.

What if I wake up and Diane isn't there? What if I keep waking up and finding myself in another dream? Where does it end?

I grab a dressing gown and wrap it around me as I run for the door, slamming it shut behind me. I head down the hall, half running, half stumbling, convinced that I can hear the bat-thing following me.

I check the bathroom and the spare rooms, but there is still no sign of Diane. And realistically, why should there be? This is my dream. There's no reason on Earth that she would need to turn up for it.

Downstairs, there's no one in the living room, everything is quiet. Silent as the grave.

I'm hitting light switches as I go, but the house still seems dark and I know I'm wasting my time. I need to wake up. I need to somehow find the courage to wake up.

I stop running. I try to stop panicking.

I stand still and close my eyes, waiting for the bat to come for me. Nothing happens.

And when I open my eyes again I'm back in bed. It's 3.00am. I'm still alone.

Slowly, I throw back the duvet and walk to the wardrobe. When I open it there's no sign of a bat, there's no trace of the paper clippings.

"It's all over. There is no future," a voice inside my head that isn't mine tells me.

I draw back the curtains and there, in the back garden, illuminated in the moonlight is Diane. She's standing out there on the grass, naked and motionless, in the middle of the lawn, her back to me, her arms outstretched like a crucifixion.

I grab my dressing gown again and run through the house, ignoring the lights, down the stairs, through the kitchen, through the open back door and only then do I slow down.

"Diane?" I ask, hardly knowing if I expect an answer.

I walk toward her, knowing deep down that this isn't just another dream. This is reality whether I like it or not.

"Sweetheart?" I almost daren't get any closer. She just stands there, like a statue.

I finally move round to the front of her, expecting the worst, expecting her to have had her eyes pecked out by the bat-thing in the wardrobe, expecting her to have blood running from her mouth or a hole in her chest where her heart should be.

But she's fine. Totally uninjured, her eyes open and staring straight ahead. I try to lower her arms, but they're rigid and cold as marble. There's no telling how long she's been standing here like this. "Diane," I whisper, "can you hear me?"

Sleepwalking? Is that it?

I try to remember what it is you're supposed to do. Never wake a sleepwalker, right? But I don't think anyone ever really told me what to do in a situation like this.

She hardly appears to be breathing.

Something flutters in a tree off to my left, something I'm hoping is an owl or just your everyday, normal, non-vampire bat. And whilst I'm looking around for a clue as to what I should do, she speaks.

"Julian?" So quiet, so soft.

"Yes, it's me, Babe." And I'm pulling my dressing gown off and draping it awkwardly over her. She still won't drop her arms.

"Why am I in the garden? Why can't I move my arms?"

I stroke her cheek and she's freezing, even though it's not that cold a night. Her skin almost feels hard to the touch.

"Try to relax. You've been sleepwalking."

She relaxes a little bit too much. Suddenly her legs just give way and she's on the grass lying there, sprawled on the dew covered lawn.

I kneel beside her and lift her head. She still seems half asleep. "We need to get you inside."

"But I'm so tired, Julian. Can't I sleep here? With you?"

Her voice is like she's dreaming, but right there, as I'm leaning over her, trying to pick her up, I feel her move beneath me, and she's arching her back and smiling, and her hand has moved to my groin and she's stroking me and, despite my best efforts to remain calm, she's making me hard.

"Come on, babe," I'm telling her. "You're cold! Let's get inside then you can do whatever you want." Let's get you to bed. Get you to sleep.

"Don't you want me, Julian? I can make you hard, can't I? Look! I can make you come. Just like your mummy did."

My spine turns to ice and I feel like if I move even an inch it will shatter into a million pieces, crippling me right there on the lawn. She's stroking me, lying there with her eyes closed, smiling and rubbing my cock, which keeps getting harder.

"I can be your mummy, Julian. You'd like that wouldn't you?" Suddenly she opens her eyes wide, staring right at me and I reel backward as she catches me off balance and I'm lying on my back on the wet grass and she's on top of me, the dressing gown flapping in a sudden breeze, her breasts inches from my face as she holds my hands above my head.

"This isn't funny, Diane!"

She puts her mouth close to my ear and whispers, "Call me "mummy", Julian. I want you to fuck me like you used to fuck her."

And as I lie there she shifts her weight and manages somehow to get me inside her and then I'm trapped again, she's holding me down as she bucks her pelvis, and she's whispering all the time, uttering things she'd never normally say.

And it's all so wrong. The way she's forcing me, it isn't right, but I'm harder tonight than I've been in years she pulls my head up and forces a breast against my mouth. She's yelling out orders, telling me what to do. "Suck on mummy's nipples, Julian!" And I do, I can't help myself and for a split second I find myself back with Jenny. In an instant, everything about Diane changes, her hair, her body, her voice.

Just for a second it's Jenny on top of me, whispering obscenities, asking me to fuck her, to rape her, to violate everything she is. And there on my lawn, I explode inside her and I'm not sure if this is 1995 or 1975. I want so much to believe that this is real, and as I calm down, my erection falling away, I'm no longer even sure who it is that collapses into my arms.

I lie there for a while, my eyes closed, and that smell, Jen's smell, is reaching my nostrils, tempting me. Before I know what's happening she's moving herself around, sitting above me, lowering herself onto my face as I begin to lick at her, tasting her again after so long, I pull her to me, gripping her thighs tightly as I push my tongue deep inside her and, as the minutes pass, as she uses her mouth to make me hard again, the muscles in her legs tighten and she clamps my head between her thighs and my ears start to ring as the pressure is suddenly too much-

-and when I open my eyes again it's bright sunshine and the birds are singing and I'm in the middle of the lawn alone. I'm naked, my dressing gown out of reach, strewn across a nearby rose bush. As far as I can tell it's early Friday morning and as I stumble to my feet I notice the curtains twitch at the bedroom of the house next door. My head hurts and I feel like I've been out drinking.

The back door is still wide open and I retrieve my dressing gown and walk back into the house without even bothering to put it on.

As I'm closing the door behind me I can hear someone coming down the stairs and, irrationally embarrassed, I instinctively hold the gown in front of me to try and cover my nudity.

"I woke up and you weren't there."

It takes me a while in my current, confused state to work out if those words were said by her or by me.

From her questioning look, I'm guessing it wasn't me. I sit down at the kitchen table and drape my dressing gown over my lap.

"I think I must have been sleepwalking, or something."

She comes over, pulls round a chair and sits beside me, putting a hand on my shoulder and remarking on how cold I feel.

"Julian, is everything okay?" And I just stare at her blankly, still not sure what to make of the images floating around in my head. "Between us, I mean."

I nod. "Everything's fine. I've just had a few things on my mind lately. Obviously things are getting to me."

Can I be certain of anything anymore? Was anyone out there with me last night? Did anything really happen? It all seemed so real at the time.

And she looks back, worried, and picks some blades of grass from my shoulder and back. "Did you sleep outside?"

And I look at her and her dressing gown is gaping open and her right breast is clearly visible and staring back at me, about two inches above her nipple is a tattoo, a stylized sunburst in black ink.

"How long have you had that tattoo? I haven't noticed it before." And she laughs and tells me, "Almost forever! Viv did it for me, back when we were together. You've seen it often enough!"

And I stand up, shaking my head and thinking how strange it is, because Diane has a tattoo just like that. No, Jenny had a tattoo just like that. And for a minute I just can't think straight. I'm so confused. I can't understand why Jenny has dyed her hair and just as I start to wonder where the hell I am, the floor beneath me seems to disappear and everything goes bla–

1995 – 1996

Television audiences bid a fond farewell this year to the popular television show, *Murder, She Wrote*, staring Angela Lansbury as the fiction-writing, crime sleuth, Jessica Fletcher.

After nearly thirteen years and more than two hundred and sixty episodes, Ms Fletcher finally decides to hang up her typewriter and settle down in Cabot Cove where she can enjoy her pension in peace and quiet. Following her retirement, the residents of the quaint little fishing village breathe a collective sigh of relief as crime statistics fall to almost negligible levels after thirteen years of weekly murders and assaults.

Jessica Fletcher, who had been middle-aged since reaching puberty, suffered from the strange affliction of 'criminal magnetosis', which resulted in her attracting crime no matter which part of the world she was currently residing in. When Jessica Fletcher goes to New York, Cabot Cove is safe, but New York suddenly encounters its worst crime-wave for decades. When she visits the Caribbean on holiday, so do most of the world's terrorists.

She used to hang around with a sheriff who looked a lot like Howard Cunningham from Happy Days, and who had remarked on more than one occasion that "Jessica could find murder on the moon." Perhaps if the sheriff had actually locked her up instead of cracking on to her every week hundreds of innocent lives could have been saved.

Criminal Magnetosis is quite common in the land of television.

Jonathan and Jennifer Hart suffered with it for years and the wizened old biddy, Miss Marple was a walking invitation for the Grim Reaper to come calling on folks, scythe in hand.

We can only hope that one day a cure can be found.

5 July 1996
... Slip Inside the Eye of Your Mind

"You know how it is, Doctor, I'm taking my medicine, I'm resting and I'm ignoring the other patients when they tell me I'm insane. I don't know what else I can do to prove to you that I'm perfectly well again!"

Doctor Hussein looks at me and then at the pencil he's holding, which he waves around as he talks, living out his personal fantasy that he's a world famous conductor for the London Philharmonic. "Julian, we've been having this discussion every week now for months. We begin with me telling you that you're making progress, you then tell me you're perfectly fine now and want to go home but, during subsequent questioning we discover that you still want to go looking for your mother."

"Everyone needs their mum from time to time, doc."

"Yes, Julian, but according to your wife, you told her that your mother died when you were a young child."

Oh, he has a point. He always has a point. That, I suppose, is why he's a highly paid psychiatric doctor and I'm a lowly, unpaid mental patient. But this time I've got my answers all worked out. This time he'll have no choice but to release me.

"Well, she did die, Doctor Hussein, she did. I understand that now and just want to let you know that I'm definitely not going to go looking for her when I get out of here. That would be a really stupid thing for me to try and do."

The doctor makes some notes, scratches absently at the side of his cheek then holds up one of those ink-blot test cards. "Tell me what you see when you look at this card, Julian."

Now, this one is easy. Over the past few weeks he's held up loads of these cards and I've told him exactly what he wants to hear. It's a pretty, colourful butterfly, it's a sheep, happily munching grass in a field, it's a teddy bear. This one looks like blood spraying from the neck of a virgin that's being bitten by Dracula and the blood has fallen in the shape of a rabid dog with huge fangs.

"I see a man patting a small fluffy dog. A poodle, I think. Yes, definitely a poodle, I can see it better now. And the poodle has a bow in its hair. I think it's a blue one."

And again he scribbles something on his pad and although I'm having to read upside-down and the pad's at a bit of an angle to me, it looks like *possible latent homosexual urges and/or sexual attraction to animals esp. dogs*. And he's underlined homosexual whilst smiling at me in a way I'm not overly comfortable with.

But then again, I may have read it wrong. I'm just a mental patient after all.

"All right Julian, I want you to put yourself in a situation and tell me how you'd react. Tell me how the situation would make you feel, okay?"

"Okay." We've done all this before too. We play the game again, Doctor.

"You're having a day out in a park, walking past a pond with your mother."

"My mum's dead, Doctor." You don't catch me there, you sneaky bastard.

"Just for the purposes of this exercise, let's pretend she's still alive."

"Isn't that what got me stuck in here in the first place?"

He smiles and decides to revise the question.

"Imagine you're in a park, having a walk with your wife."

"Who isn't my mother." I add helpfully.

"That's right. You're passing by a pond filled with ducks and birds and she's brought some bread to feed to them. There are three different birds nearby, a mallard, a goose and a swan. What do you do next?"

"I put up an umbrella."

"Why?"

"It's raining. The forecast said it was possible and it looked a bit grey and cloudy when we left the house so I pickled one up. It's a blue one." Nice colour, blue. It's calm, soothing, has none of the negative connotations of red or green.

"Ok. I was more looking to find out which of the three birds you feed first. "

I scratch at my head and stroke my chin, regretting that recently I've shaved my beard off. They said it was getting too long and that too much food was getting caught in it so they told me to get rid of it before they tied me down and did it for me.

"What birds were they again?"

"A mallard, a goose and a swan."

"And what's the mallard look like?"

"It's just a duck. A duck with a green head, if you like."

"So there's a duck, a goose and a swan?"

"Yes."

"And you want me to feed one?"

"Yes."

I give him a slight pause to show how much I think these days. "Which one represents my mother? Because if I know that then I can ignore it, because she's dead and that will make it easier because then I'll only have two birds to choose between."

It's probably the Mallard. It's got a green head, probably supposed to signify envy. Like I'm envious of my father because he got to sleep with my mother. If I chose the Mallard, I probably get another year added to my stay here.

Doctor Hussein doesn't seem overly impressed, but then I have little sympathy since he gets paid just for sitting here talking to me. Gets paid quite a lot I expect. For me, this is just volunteer work.

"Julian, every week we go through this sort of behaviour. Every week you try to convince me that you aren't obsessed with your dead mother by constantly talking about her. You keep trying to convince me you're well, but I'm sorry, I'm just not believing what you're telling me."

Damn. I can never beat this guy. Next week I'll remember not to mention my mother, though then he'll want to know why I'm repressing her memory. I suppose I could just time myself and only mention her every five minutes or so, that might convince him I'm okay. Then he'll think I'm doing it on purpose, making out I'm fine when I'm not. Tell you what, next week, at the session, I'll only talk about my father. That will work. He's alive and well and knows I'm not insane. But then he'll think I've got one of those complex things, where a guy fancies his own father and maybe kills his father because he can't find a way to make the relationship work and then he'll keep me here even longer and he'll write more of those notes and my file will just keep getting bigger and bigger and

"I'm not gay, you know."

And Doctor Hussein is silent for a while, thinking carefully before scribbling what I'm sure is the word denial next to his previous 'homosexual' comment. Suddenly I find that I'm hugging my arms around my chest and swaying gently back and forth. I'm no longer sure there's a way out of this for me today.

"No." He says. "I think we should move the discussion on to other areas that are beginning to concern me."

Oh, he has more concerns. I'm going to be here for years at this rate. "Was it the swan?" I ask.

"What?"

"The swan. Was I supposed to feed the swan?"

"That doesn't matter anymore, Julian."

"*Doesn't matter?* Won't it get hungry?"

"It swam away. Someone else fed the swan."

"Someone who isn't insane, no doubt. Go on Doc, you can tell me the truth."

"Julian, is it true that you told one of the patients that you're from the future? That you came back in time to stop your younger self doing stupid things?"

That would be James. I told him that in confidence.

"I never said that, Doctor. I think someone is trying to make you think that I'm insane."

"Julian, please don't use the word 'insane', we prefer to say that the patients here are 'ill'."

"You're telling me! That James Connerby thinks he's Tom Cruise and that he's been replaced by an alien body snatcher who's going round Hollywood making crap films he'd never sign up to in a million years. Now that's what I call mental. Sorry, 'ill'."

It's all so easy to accuse me of being crazy, with your PhD and certificates on the wall. Wait 'til I show you my 2003 pound coin, that will prove a few things. Or it would, but now I think about it, I got really drunk one night a few years back and used it to buy fishcake and chips. I've often regretted that.

"And did you know that the patients want to put on a panto this year? They figure that because they have an actor like Tom Cruise here, they can get him to play Aladdin and really get the Christmas spirit flowing."

"That sounds like it might be fun. Are you going to be in it?"

"They want me to play Widow Twanky."

Instantly he writes on his pad *cross-dressing* and looks back at me smiling and showing too many teeth. "Are you going to do it?"

It's almost a dare! Oh, go on, Julian, please dress up as a woman and prove that you secretly like boys. I'm not falling for this!

"I'm afraid, not. I'm otherwise ... committed."

Plus they want to stage it next month, which is hardly enough time to get ready for a play, not to mention the insanity of having a panto more than four months before Christmas! The bloody lunatics!

"So you never told James that you come from 2006?"

He likes this line of questioning. I'm going to have to cover myself carefully here.

"No."

It's the best I can do at such short notice. Deny everything.

"Your wife tells us that she still hasn't managed to locate your birth certificate or any record of your National Insurance number. We've checked with local authorities in Leicester and there's no record of you ever attending school there."

"Public records, eh? Always losing things. At least now that everything is stored on computer there'll be less chance of things getting lost."

Doctor Hussein has started doodling on the pad. Next to his notes about me he appears to have sketched a woman with unfeasibly large breasts and eighteen inches of erect penis.

"And then there's the matter of your age. Your wife tells us that she first met you in nineteen seventy-one when you were, she thought, about thirty years old, which should make you about fifty-five now?"

Actually it's more like sixty-odd, but who's counting? "I've always looked young for my age."

"You look, particularly since you lost the beard, to be in your thirties. Can you explain that to me?"

"No."

"Julian," he's getting aggressive now, like a hunter, his prey in sight, ready to launch his final attack and bring home the bacon, "I put it to you that you are, in fact, from the twenty-first century and, much in the style of the film, Twelve Monkeys you have come back to the past and been locked up as you appear to be insane, but are in actuality here to save the future."

"I'm sorry, Doctor, I can't possibly comment."

And two of the orderlies have moved into position behind him as he gets more and more worked up.

"I'm sorry, Doctor Hussein, but it looks like our session is over." And I stand up and let the orderlies drag the good 'doctor' off for his weekly appointment with Doctor Evangelis where he'll probably be heavily sedated before being kept in isolation for the next week.

I check the clock and note that my meeting with Evangelis isn't until next Wednesday, so I have plenty of time ahead of me to plan my answers to the real doctor's questions.

I wander over to join a game of snakes and ladders monopoly that's being played, a clever little amalgam where you build houses and hotels for the snakes to live in and they pay rent and eat your enemies. On the way over I stop to ask James if he's aware that his body double has just released a film remake of the *Mission Impossible* television series.

"That's so fucking lame, man," he tells me in his heavy West Midlands brogue. "I told my agent I only do Shakespeare from now on!"

James Connerby is a forty-six year old television repair man from Birmingham who is in here for developing a mad obsession with everything Tom Cruise. He is currently waiting for his wife, Nicole to post bail and get him out. The last anyone heard was that

Nicole Kidman and Tom Cruise had both filed for injunctions preventing Connerby from calling their house or writing them fan mail or even being in the same country as them.

And once again I remain trapped in a world of mental patients, biding my time and endlessly searching for the way back home.

As the Beatles once said, 'It's getting better all the time.'

1996 – 1997

In the passing of just a quarter of a century the world has seen the emergence of space shuttles, home computers that rivalled the computing power of the Hal 9000 and the invention of the DVD. We've seen a new era of East-West relations and enlightened views toward race and sexuality. The world is ready for the next mammoth leap forward in humanity's grand design, waiting with awe to see where the next few years would lead.

Enter the Teletubbies.

These multi-coloured, gibberish-talking creatures emerged as the next evolutionary step for mankind. Originally designed to educate babies and children, the Teletubbies actually appealed more to the student population where they were considered to be role models and oh, so trendy.

This new version of the Fab Four consisted of the yellow one, Laa-Laa, lime-green Dipsy, bright red Po and the ragingly homosexual, purple-assed Tinky-Winky.

In actuality, Tinky-Winky was the only straight one in the group and used his paycheques to fund an almost endless procession of Taiwanese prostitutes. He only carried the handbag for a dare and the whole thing kind of backfired on him, much to the amusement of his fellow Tubbies.

Creator of the Teletubbies, an evil genetic scientist called Anne Wood, also created the Boohbahs, a group of colourful, gibberish-talking aliens called Humbah, Zumbah, Jumbah, Jingbah and Zing Zing Zingbah. Oh, and she was also responsible for Pob, a mostly incomprehensible puppet that used to spit all over the camera and write his name in the mess.

Honestly. It makes you wish they'd bring back Rainbow.

1 May 1997
... I'm a Million Different People

Some days are better than others when you're committed and life at St Christian's 'Home for the Emotionally Troubled' has its fair share of ups and downs. I've been in here for a while now and everyone says that I'm getting better, though apparently I still have days when I think Jenny is alive and I sometimes claim she comes to visit and says 'hi' to me in my room.

As I sit here, looking out of the window at the other patients in the garden, I find it hard to believe that I'm ill at all. I have no personal recollection of these 'visions' I keep having and, as far as I can tell, seem to be perfectly well. I'm certainly closer to being released than Kirsty, the girl they admitted about six months ago. She's out there now, sitting on a bench by the wall talking to four stones she carries around in the pocket of her dressing gown.

Kirsty's house burned down one day when she was out at the shops.

She left her four kids at home to fend for themselves and someone started playing with matches and the next thing, everyone in the house was dead.

She's under the impression that the stones contain the spirits of her children. Don't ask me why, I'm not a psychiatrist.

When I compare myself to her, I'm not sure why I'm here at all.

When I look at all the other patients in the day room, I'm almost certain I'm the only sane drop in an ocean of madness.

Roger thinks he's a retired Formula One driver, James still thinks he's Tom Cruise, Harry has some sort of problem being in the same city as other people and rumour has it that Ernie likes to masturbate in the frozen poultry sections of large supermarkets.

I really don't see why it's so wrong for me to fantasise about being in a relationship with my dead mother, but then I am under some pretty strong medication these days.

The day room is quite crowded this afternoon and even the chronically depressed patients and bed-wetters have been allowed to join in as we host our own version of the United Kingdom General Election. Today will see the Labour Party gain power in Britain for the first time since the seventies and in view of the fact that most of the people in here can't really nip out to the polling station, we've decided to hold our own little in-house vote. Just to let all us nutters think we're part of the outside world.

So, for therapeutic reasons, the doctors here have given us the go ahead to hold elections for Prime Minister of the Day Room. It's a much sought after post and the past seven days have been filled will the four candidates wandering around, trying to find out which way you were going to vote. The shortlist of candidates was picked by Doctor Evangelis and the senior nursing staff and each one was told to behave like a politician for a week and the winner would be Prime Minister for a while and get all the associated perks like extra puddings and a long lie-in on Sunday mornings.

The patient selected to be the Conservative candidate was Ian Stables, a kleptomaniac who's been locked up in here for years. Occasionally Ian has been let out, but invariably steals something within twenty-four hours of release and is sent back for further observation. He's sort of the big boss-man around here and has been given the responsibility of filling the rightwing position. His campaign promises have mainly been that if you vote for him, he won't steal your stuff. At least not for a while, anyway.

Left-wing opposition has been handed to Lydia Tennant, an ex-primary school teacher from Derby who was committed after being found locked in a stationery cupboard muttering 'the bastards, the bastards' over and over again. Apparently unable to stop herself screaming when being within line of sight of anyone under the age of eleven, Lydia's teaching days are long over and she's been mainly campaigning on the 'bring back child labour' ticket, though it is thought that her slightly more radical 'enforced euthanasia for kids' policies may lose her some of the younger votes.

Thirdly, the sit-on-the-fence, middle-of-the-road, never-getting-into-power-so-don't -have-to- follow-through-on-any-of-our-campaign-promises candidate is Sarah Weaver. Sarah was arrested after a nasty incident concerning Howard from Take That. The details are sketchy, but as far as anyone can tell, Sarah was something of a stalker and made claims that she was the mother of Howard's lovechild. Police arrested her outside the star's house, where she was waiting for him to come back from a world tour and was attempting to breast feed a Mr Potato Head doll that she kept referring to as 'Little Howie'.

Playing for the Liberals, Sarah has promised that under her domination there will be a complete abolition of all forms of taxation and that overcrowding in prisons will be solved by ordering the release of fifty percent of the better behaved criminals.

Last and probably least is Craig 'Popeye' Doyle, the Independent candidate. Many have speculated that Craig took his name from Gene Hackman's character in *The French Connection*, but they'd be wrong. 'Popeye' was a nickname he picked up because he liked dressing up as a sailor and roaming the docks looking for sexual favours. His repeated offences eventually led to a trial at which he blamed all his problems on the day he caught his father in bed with a man who looked just like Captain Birdseye. The judge took pity on him and sent him here for three months observation where, despite the best efforts of the medical staff, he continues to wear a sailor's hat.

Also, in spite of Doctor Evangelis' best recommendations, Craig insists on calling himself the Monster Raving Loony Party and has maintained that under his government each and every person over the age of eighteen will receive a free Tinky-Winky doll, to do with as they please.

It's been a hard fought battle this last week and, though I'm still not sure if their policies are any better or worse than those proposed by the actual, real-life, election candidates, I did my duty and voted for Sarah Weaver on the basis that she was the youngest, best-looking candidate and could regularly be seen nursing Mr Potato Head if you knew where to look.

Three hours later and the votes have all been counted and the winner's party is in full swing. Everyone has a glittery hat and one of those things you blow into that makes a noise and rolls out to make it look like you've got an exceptionally long tongue with a feather stuck on the end. Everyone has their choice of red, orange or green jelly and no one gives a sod about how the real election is going on outside.

The St Christian's voting system resulted in something of a landslide as Doctor Evangelis read out the results, having first explained that there was something of a mix up in the counting, but everything was sorted out now.

It seems that Ian failed to generate much interest and gained only five votes, most people being of the opinion that simply being voted in as Prime Minister wasn't enough to stop him nicking all your belongings.

Third place went to Craig with twenty-three votes, who was secretly relieved that he didn't have to shell out on Teletubby dolls for everyone.

The runner's up position went to Lydia, with a staggering forty-six votes, which was the first indication that something was amiss, since there were only around a hundred voters in the hospital, leaving only twenty-odd votes for Sarah.

And Sarah was declared the winner with four thousand, nine hundred and fifty-four votes, which was no mean feat and involved me sitting up all night, marking up ballot papers and stuffing them into the voting box without being seen.

As always, justice in the world of politics is served and corruption always wins the day, regardless of who the poll-going public actually voted for.

1997 – 1998

Whilst it's not everyone's ambition to end up in a mental hospital, spending your days staring into space or playing cards with your imaginary friends and losing, some would argue that, by and large, it's a better place to be than the real world where things just keep getting weirder and no one ever offers you an explanation for anything.

There's a lot of speculation around the passing of Princess Diana in Paris, whose tragic death at a fairly young age has brought into question the oppressive role of the media in its ceaseless pursuit of celebrities. More than that, the sanity of the British public is again doubted as, starved of good storylines in *Coronation Street* or *EastEnders*, they invent their own conspiracy theories that Diana was assassinated by order of the Queen and then demand that because she was really, really nice, she should be made into a Saint.

But time moves long and things continue to get worse as 'action hero', Steven Seagal is declared to be a reincarnated Buddhist lama, little known terrorist, Osama Bin Laden issues a fatwa against pretty much anyone living west of Afghanistan and the music world proves that artificial boy bands are no longer the way forward as the Eurovision Song Contest is won by an artificial girl, the Israeli transsexual, Dana International.

All of this in a year that sees the release of Viagra, another football World Cup that England doesn't win, and George Michael dropping a few 'careless whispers' in LA's public toilets. And just what in God's name is *Quidditch*?

31 May 1998
... Showtime

After more than two and a half years in St Christian's I'm finally being released and waiting for Diane to come and pick me up. I've said a tearful goodbye to Doctor Evangelis and Doctor Sorrell, who were both instrumental in nursing me back to full mental health, as was Doctor Hussein in his own special way. I've also said my final goodbyes to my fellow patients, many of which will never recover and will have to live out the remainder of their existence as hopeless mental cases.

Like James Connerby, one of the people I'd become close friends with during my stay. Still believing himself to be Tom Cruise, he has now formed his own movie company made up entirely of patients from the hospital who think they're famous movie stars. Amazingly he's so far managed to get a line up of A-list celebs like Brad Pitt, Leonardo DiCaprio and Bruce Willis. He's even found one guy who claims to be the reincarnation of the not-yet-dead Winona Ryder.

On the other side of the hall, waving goodbye, is the 'Rings' brigade.

These are some of the more bizarre lifers and long-term patients. These guys think that they're all characters from Lord of the Rings and have a set hierarchical order to which all involved must adhere. Bill Ramsey, or 'Dark Lord Sauron', as he prefers to be called, is the leader. He's been here since sometime in the sixties. Beneath him are his deputies, Tom Bronson and Alan Dillon, who are the wizards Gandalf and Saruman respectively.

On the next tier down are a load of guys claiming to be elves, below them the dwarfs and at the bottom of the pile as always, the hobbits.

These complete lemons hold meetings every week where they discuss plans to escape from St Christian's and take over 'Middle Earth' using the shower curtain ring they stole from the bathroom. They hold practice fights amongst themselves so they know exactly what they're going to be doing on the outside. The sight of Bill, now almost seventy years old, standing there with his hands outstretched shouting, 'Whoosh! Zap! You're all dead! Bow down before the might of Sauron!" is enough to consign him here for the rest of his unnatural life.

On the plus side, some of the elves manage to die quite well when they get shot. It's all really quite artistic.

So I wave goodbye to all the 'ill' people, the comical, the depressives, the kleptomaniacs, the people too scared to sleep and the people too scared to wake up. And although part of me will miss the place, a mental hospital is definitely no place to spend large parts of your life wallowing around.

Diane picks me up in a new red Mercedes and we hug like crazy until I eventually put her down and climb into the passenger seat. She's been to see me every month since I've been ill and I know it hasn't been easy for her, seeing me either out of my mind or sedated. A lesser woman would have taken the money and run. Not my Diane.

When I first went away I told her she didn't have to wait, that she could do anything she wanted to whilst I was away. She told me then that all she wanted to do was watch me getting better. I'm not sure she expected it to take nearly three years, but I'm here now and she's still around, and if she's done anything with anyone else whilst I was recovering I told her it's ok, I just don't want to hear about it.

From time to time I've kept up with events in the world, so as not to be a complete stranger to it when I finally got released. During my time away the country now has its New Labour government, Hong Kong has gone back to the Chinese, (though I don't think the Chinese ever really believed it was British), Scotland has voted for its own parliament, and Princess Diana and Mother Teresa have both died. I'm also glad to note that during my time in the hospital, the world hasn't destroyed itself in a nuclear war and that mankind is not yet dominated by machines. With all the Earth-changing news I've missed over the past couple of years it's somewhat of an anticlimax when the newspaper that Diane has bought me to commemorate my homecoming greets me with the news that *'Ginger Spice Quits! Pop World in Ruins!'*

"The companies are doing fine." She tells me as we drive the ten miles or so back to the house. Since I've been in hospital Diane has given up the hairdressing salon and taken on the running of the investment empire. There's not actually much to run, but she at least kept an eye on the management companies and brokers and closed down some of the more 'legally ambiguous' companies that may not have been actually breaking the law, but were certainly bending it into positions the government never envisaged.

"Are we still rich?"

"Richer than ever! I don't think we have to worry about money for a while. I even paid off the mortgage whilst you were gone."

Ever the businesswoman. I'll never fully understand why Pete wanted to kill her.

"So what about everyone else? Are all your friends okay? Met any new ones?"

She looks at me and grins. "Everyone's fine! And no, I didn't sleep with anyone else while you were ... ill." She squeezes my hand. "And I still can't believe how young you look without that beard!"

No, and that's odd isn't it? Her memory of me from the early seventies may be hazy, but she must have realised by now that I'm not really aging. I can't imagine why she hasn't noticed.

Well, it's best to just go with the flow, I suppose. Make the most of things and pray that I don't relapse. I genuinely haven't dreamed about Jenny for months. I can talk about her now without getting weird and nothing has been scratching at my window in the early hours of the morning.

We arrive at the house and I realise that I'm feeling more than a little subdued. It's been a long time since I was last here and it almost feels like someone else's home. Diane takes me around each room, pointing out new additions, showing me how she's changed furniture and bought new ornaments and it's almost like I'm viewing the house for the first time, with Diane as my estate agent.

Eventually we reach the bedroom and I sit on the bed, immediately amazed at how soft it feels compared to the hospital bed I've grown so used to.

And though it feels like I've spent the last three years of my life resting, I still feel the need to sleep for a while.

Diane kisses me on the forehead and tells me she'll be downstairs if I want anything. And I just lie on top of the duvet, close my eyes and fall asleep in my own bed.

1998 – 1999

The final nails are hammered into the coffin of quality television as someone in the Netherlands finally invents the reality TV show, *Big Brother* and the way is paved for endless hours of cheap programming and media hype.

Take a dozen nobodies, put them in a house and film everything they do. Systematically evict the character that provides the least entertainment and give the survivor at the end of the series loads of cash and probably a record deal, irrespective of whether they can sing or not.

The format has been duplicated in over forty countries from Thailand to Ecuador and hopes still ride high that a special 'Vatican City' series will be broadcast in which a bunch of cardinals are put together and the one who makes it to the end without ordering out for a choir-boy gets to be the next Pope.

Each year the Big Brother phenomenon is added to by newspapers and magazines who suddenly find that the illegal invasion of Middle Eastern countries gets nowhere near as many readers as a story about why certain houseguests need to win the prize money so they can get tit-implants.

A recent survey asked the working classes what they thought of George Orwell's vision of the elite controlling the populace through constant observation and media propaganda. The question was met with a puzzled silence.

Forty-seven percent of people quizzed thought that George Orwell was to be a guest on the next series of *Celebrity Big Brother*. Sixty-two percent thought he directed the porn film, *Animal Farm*.

One hundred percent of *Big Brother* viewers questioned regularly purchased *Heat* magazine.

16 September 1999
... Everything He Lacks, Well He Makes Up In Denial

I've been back home for just over a year and I've already completely screwed up almost every facet of my life. As the nineties draw to a close I know that whilst I was biding my time in the hospital, I've missed an important time in my younger self's life. I've completely ignored the younger Julian Grant and stayed out of his life during a time when he really could have used a good friend.

Over the last five years the man I used to be has got married, messed up his life, got divorced, messed it up some more and, after mistreating himself and several women in loveless one night stands, has finally got involved with Kieran Donnelly, which, whilst being entertaining in its own way, was one of the worst mistakes I ever made.

That was two years ago, when the young, charismatic Kieran Donnelly came into my life and took me away from all my hurt.

Kieran was something of a wild-boy, the thirty year old son of a member of parliament who paid him a handsome allowance each month to stay away from home and never let the papers know that he existed. For his part, Kieran was happy enough to take the money, though his father needn't have worried since Kieran didn't want anyone he knew finding he was the son of a Tory MP.

Kieran spent his seemingly endless supply of money in bars, restaurants and night clubs and used to love wining and dining his many male friends from the ages of fifteen to twenty-five. When I met him I was twenty-seven, but looked younger and Kieran soon took me under his wing and eventually into his bed.

I'd often found myself questioning my sexuality and whilst I never got the chance to do anything about it before meeting Kieran, I knew that I found the men featured in pornography to be just as arousing as the women. I often wondered about the things I could get up to should I ever find the right person to initiate me.

Strangely, the relationship with Kieran lasted longer and was far more sexual than the one I'd had with my wife, Samantha. We shared interests in film and literature and often went to the cinema together where, contrary to popular belief, we did not spend the whole of every film feeling each other up. Not every film.

In March this year Kieran asked the younger me if I would like to go travelling with him as he was planning to head down through Europe and over to Asia, finishing up by spending the millennium celebrations in Thailand. Being keen to see what I could of the world, I took him up on his offer and we set off on an all expenses paid trip to what turned out to be the seediest back alleyways of the world.

Kieran never had a shortage of either money or drugs and quite often we would roam the streets and bars, smashed out of our faces, looking for boys and girls to join us for the night, ones that didn't need to go back to their parents and would do almost anything provided they were assured of a free taxi home in the morning.

Kieran didn't mind at all if I wanted to bring girls back with us, though he would never get involved himself, just sit in a chair watching as I paid the girls to do anything I wanted. Occasionally he would let a girl touch him as I made him come, but he would never once consider touching them. It just wasn't his thing.

Due to Kieran's predilection for younger men, it was normally students that we ended up with and during the months we spent renting a flat in Paris, we went to many parties that always seemed to degenerate into drunken orgies. On the whole I have no complaints, though we should perhaps have been a little more wary of what we were getting into. We were careful, steered clear of major disease risks, generally had the time of our lives and, in a couple of months time, I will be spending New Years

Eve in a Bangkok hotel room with three teenaged lady-boys and more cocaine than you could possibly ever need in one night.

Kieran had the money to go anywhere and do anything he wanted. He had contacts in every major city in Europe who could supply him with any drugs he needed at an hour's notice. He had the sort of contacts that could help out when, one night in Munich, a seventeen year old German girl whose name we didn't even bother to find out came back with us and overdosed on a cocktail of cocaine and amphetamines. If it had become a police matter it's doubtful I would have ever have made it back to England. We had more drugs on us than most chemists and the girl had rope marks on her wrists and ankles from where I'd tied her to the bed. And just to add more evidence against me she was full of my semen, making a case for rape almost a certainty once the SS, or whoever it is that the German government employs to kill foreigners these days, got involved.

Kieran simply made one short phone call from his mobile and in twenty-five minutes two guys turned up, put her and her belongings into a laundry cart and took the whole problem away. We left Munich the next day and moved on to Austria where we limited the drug consumption and fortunately had no more fatalities to cover up.

I wonder again if I should go to Bangkok and join Julian for the millennium celebrations. On balance of things, I've pretty much decided to stay out of my other self's life now until he meets Cassie, which, having missed out on all my other opportunities to set him straight, is about the only thing left that I can try to prevent him messing up.

I'll satisfy myself knowing that, on New Year's Eve, whilst I'm getting drunk in England and trying desperately to get someone to sleep with me, my other self will already be waking up on New Year's Morning, finding the suicide note and the money and then discovering Kieran with his wrists sliced open in the bath.

It turned out that Kieran was dying of some sort of cancer and had only a few months to live. That was what his year of travelling had been about, living out the remains of his life, spending money and having fun. Ultimately choosing his own place and time to die.

I try to work out where I am now, probably in Germany, having what I think is the time of my life, not knowing that I'm just a few months away from losing Kieran in addition to all the others.

I try to work out where Diane is now, but that one is a little outside my scope.

When I came back from hospital it was like we were different people.

She'd spent nearly three years away from me and now she had to somehow fit me back into her life. She had in fact been seeing someone else. She told me about it one night a couple of months ago. She said she just needed someone to get her through the time that I was away. She'd thought it was just casual sex and companionship and when I came home it was always said that he and she would break it off. They found they couldn't and I got more difficult to get along with and she finally told me that my not getting any older was really starting to freak her out. Eventually she couldn't take any more, I started sleeping in the spare room and when I woke up this morning she had gone.

I have the money to hire someone to find her, but what's the point?

Another relationship ends, another woman lets me down. After being apart for three years she's probably closer to this Will bloke than to me anyway. And he was there for her, to look after her whilst I was doing my *Cuckoo's Nest* thing.

I made sure that she had enough money to set herself up and live comfortably with her new man. She had certainly earned enough by running my companies while I was away. And I didn't fight her as she left, I just told her that I hoped she'd be happy. I honestly meant it when I said that she deserves better than me.

There were a couple of things I never did tell her, though.

I didn't tell her about the dreams of Jenny that have returned and have been steadily getting more frequent over the past couple of months. And I didn't tell her that I'd started to see a strange, silver-blue angel standing in the corner of the room every time I turned out the lights.

Millennium

1999 – 2000

Imagine the mixture of surprise and horror as the US Presidential Election campaign gets underway and people are watching the news as the candidates head off to lie to the voting public and folks turn to one another and say "My, isn't that George Bush looking young these days."

And then you realise the awful truth that there are two George Bushes and this one doesn't appear to know from one day to the next exactly what it is he's supposed to do or say.

Still recovering from recent events in which the previous President, Bill Clinton could lie under oath, get impeached and still come out smelling of roses, the voters headed off to the polls to make their choice for his replacement.

And the results were; Al Gore: 48.4%, George II: 47.9% and some people no-one had ever heard of: 2.1 %. So it's a resounding win for Al Gore with a majority of half a million votes.

But Al Gore is apparently a Godless Communist who probably has fantasies about threesomes with Saddam Hussein and Osama Bin Laden, so George calls in a few favours from the Almighty Dad and, some Florida recounts later, George is declared the winner and Christians everywhere breathe a sigh of relief, safe in the knowledge that with God's right-hand man on the throne, those pesky Muslims will be put in their place and will never try to do bad anything against the crusading might of America.

George Junior would go on to achieve great things whilst in office such as the rejection of the Kyoto climate proposals, his complete failure to bring Osama Bin Laden to justice, and finishing off his daddy's work in Iraq with or without the backing of the United Nations.

7 November 2000
... Watching, Waiting, Commiserating

In the blink of an eye we're back here again. The year 2000 and, new millennium or not, the gateway to a bright, new, shiny future. Again I watched as everyone woke up on New Year's Day and looked out of their windows expecting for some reason that everything would be different, that the world would have been turned all silver and chrome and that finally, we had all been given the flying cars that the governments of the world were keeping under wraps.

But the world hasn't really changed, not in any major, noticeable way.

No, all we've gained from this bright new age is yet more reality television and the end of the Concorde.

And whilst I still look like a sprightly thirty-six year old man in the prime of his life, I am now, in actual fact, sixty-six years old and beginning to get more than a little pissed off with my life.

To be honest, the six years from 2000 to 2006 were difficult enough to live through once and this time round it's not even historically interesting. To combat the problems of living in a world in which millions of people are going on about how great this *Big Brother* show is, I've taken to drinking more than I should and one day last week I actually bought an axe specifically so I could smash it into the TV screen when my hate-levels finally rise too high. I shouldn't get so wound up. I should learn to be content with life as it is, improve on my already second-to-none ability to be nothing more than a spectator.

I've calculated that I now have enough money to easily see me through the next six years and have closed down all my companies, much to my advisors' consternation. The gaps I leave in the web will soon close up as other companies move in to take control of the share I've left behind. The online pornography business has given me a great living over the years, but it's time to stop playing the game and start cruising toward the finish line.

Not that I'm throwing in the towel completely, there are still some places that I want to go before I reach this mythical crisis point I've been looking forward to for so long. Next year, I want to be in New York when the towers come down and although I doubt I can do anything to stop it, I'll still try my hardest and might even be able to help out in some way. After that, from 2002 I'll have my work cut out for me making sure my other self doesn't totally fuck things up with Cassie Barclay.

I'm wandering through the house in the dark and I've drunk almost a full bottle of scotch and I'm generally wallowing around, lamenting that after re-living thirty years of my life I've wound up exactly where I was at the start, drunk and alone, with my dreams plagued by angels who never tell me anything.

It's then that hear something.

At first I listen hard, expecting to hear more scratching sounds from some dark corner, but it's not that. It's like someone throwing pebbles at my windows. I head to the back door and there on the lawn, throwing pebbles at my windows, is someone I haven't seen for a long, long time.

I start turning on lights, offer him a seat in the living room and put on the kettle to make John a coffee. I hang his battered old brown leather jacket up on the wall and stand there looking at him.

"It's been a while!" I say.

"Sure has!" He grins, showing me almost every one of his pearly white, American teeth. "You've done all right for yourself." He gestures around at the house and I nod.

"I've lost a few women along the way, but I finally made it." I look him over, and he's almost exactly the same as he was when I met him that night in the pub down in Leicester. "It's been more than twenty years! You haven't changed a bit!"

He looks at his clothes and shrugs. "Well I may need a quick shower, but the clothes are sound. And for me it's only been a few weeks since we last spoke. And you haven't exactly aged much yourself. I was worried you wouldn't remember me!"

It seems like only yesterday that him and me sat in the pub, both of us claiming to be time-travellers. Part of me always thought he'd escaped from somewhere, but there was always the mystery of that note he left, nagging away at the back of mind.

"I remember everything! So what brings you round here?"

I head into the kitchen to sort out his drink as he tells me that he's just stopping off on his way back to the states to see himself and his family when they were younger. He's not sure how good an idea that is and for once in my life I'm not lying when I say that I can totally understand where he's coming from.

I wonder if I should warn him about doing anything insane with his own mother, but in all probability I think I'm the only person I know of who's stupid enough to do that.

I hand him a hot mug and settle down on a sofa switching on the CD player which has something classical in it that tends to soothes me when the house seems too empty.

We exchange bizarre stories for the best part of five hours. He tells me things about the future as he knows it and I tell him about the stuff he missed out on from the seventies until now. He says I should look out for him on the internet soon, he wants to try and wake people up to the impending threat of World War Three and I have to explain to him that these days I don't even have a computer.

I have no reason to doubt that he's telling me the truth. He's a man out of my own past, sitting here with me now, travelling through time in a Chevy truck on a mission to save the future of all mankind. But World War Three seems a long way away and not something that I feel the need to worry about. The closer I get to 2006, the more I feel that that's as far as I'm going to go.

Don't ask me why, but again I get the impression that correcting the mistakes of my other self will be the last thing I do. That saving his life will mean the end of mine. It's just a feeling. Maybe I'm spending too much time alone in an empty house.

Eventually we exhaust our stories and he leaves and as I stand with him beside his truck, he shows me the strange black box in the back with its few flashing LEDs and dials and I wish him luck as he flicks a switch, hops into the driver's seat and just fades away into nothing.

I shake my head and wander off to my bedroom and lying there, all by myself, I notice the faint glow of the angel standing in the corner of the room watching over me. Just as she has every night since Diane left.

But she never speaks, never tells me why she's here. She just watches me and I know that by the time I wake up she'll be gone.

2000 – 2001

The twenty-first century begins in earnest and, despite widespread expectation, only one large black monolith appears overnight, in Seattle, USA. The nine-foot tall structure grants monkeys in the local zoo a heightened sense of awareness and, by lunchtime on January 1, a team of chimpanzees has constructed a working computer out of items found on the floor of their cage.

By the summer, apes have taken over most of the North Western United states and have issued warrants for the arrest of both Charlton Heston and Marky Mark, although at this time it is uncertain whether the apes are also interested in arresting other members of the infamous 'Funky Bunch'.

The ape uprising proves to be short-lived and Ape City, as Seattle is now called, is stormed by US marines and re-taken. On closer investigation, the apes were found to be nothing more than outraged Democrats in monkey suits desperately trying to cling to power in the wake of the recent Republican election victory.

Elsewhere in the world, the United Kingdom is circulating its latest census questionnaires and thousands of government officials were busy collating and amending the results to fit in with how they thought the current demographics should read.

Under the 'Religion' category there are apparently still seven out ten people claiming to be Christians, which is good news for God, and almost four hundred thousand English Jedi Knights, which is bad news for the Sith.

Sadly, despite this huge number of lightsabre wielders, being a Jedi is still not recognised as an official British religion.

11 September 2001
... Caught Up in the Conflict

Everyone remembers where they were on the day the towers came down. I was at work when someone rushed in claiming that a plane had hit the World Trade Center and by the time I got home the whole thing had collapsed. There were thousands dead and there was nothing anyone could do about it.

This time around I'd come over to America, arriving a week before the attack and, even though I knew it was futile, I spent the whole of that week calling various government departments from various call boxes, telling them that the Trade Center had to be closed down on the morning of the eleventh.

Obviously, no one listened.

I phoned the Trade Center repeatedly and asked if they were aware that terrorists were plotting to attack them. I got laughed off the phone every time.

I called the FBI again and told them about the Pentagon being a secondary target, they told me to wait where I was and someone would be around to pick me up so that we could talk about this in person.

So, despite my best efforts, on the day of the attack I was up early and was watching with the other horrified commuters as the planes came in and the towers came down.

The planes were quieter than I imagined, so high to begin with that you wouldn't know they were there unless you were looking. I can imagine the people in the Trade Center towers, sat at their desks, bored one minute, gazing out of a window, the next wondering just how close a plane can get before it alters course. When it becomes obvious that the plane isn't going to bank to the side, it's as if everyone's feet have been nailed to the floor, leaving them unable to move. And even if they could move, where exactly would they go?

I remember seeing the photos of people jumping from the tower rather than staying to burn. It's difficult to explain how it feels to actually watch them jump.

This time round, right up close to the towers, there were tears in my eyes. People around me must have thought I was mad as I punched repeatedly at the nearest wall until my knuckles were raw. Like everything else I'd seen or encountered in the past, there was nothing I could do here but watch and let history unfold.

I headed closer to the site, trying to block out the screams and the sirens, hoping that I wouldn't get held back by the police or rescue workers.

And for the whole day I'm there, helping out where I can. All day I help to shift rubble, help the injured, help the servicemen wherever they need it. But to the thousands who have lost their lives, I'm still worthless. I might as well have not been there.

I hung around the site, helping until there was nothing else to do but go back to my hotel. Having spent the day trying to get any injured people to ambulances, the smoke and dust finally became too much and, choking, I wandered back to my room to get cleaned up.

On the way to the hotel I stopped off at a phone and called the FBI to ask how they felt now? I yelled at them, screaming as I watched the smoke still rising from the crash site. I asked why they didn't listen, but all they wanted was for me to come in and help them with their enquiries. I was just trying to save lives and now I'm regarded as another suspect.

I returned to my room and watched the endless news coverage of the disaster, questioning again what the point was in being here if I can't make a single important difference.

And right now at this second as I'm lying in a strange bed in a hotel, three thousand miles from home, over on the other side of the room is the blurred, naked figure of the angel, staring at me, an indistinct amalgam of every woman I've ever known in my life.

"Why?" I ask her. "Why won't you let me change anything?"

"Hush." She says, speaking to me for the first time, her voice like a dozen different women speaking at once. "Don't worry. It's all coming to an end soon."

And though it chills me to the bone, I know she's right. There's only one thing left for me to do now.

2001 – 2002

"And so God spoke to his anointed one on Earth and told him that the ways of truth and freedom must be maintained at all costs and that all false gods and their worshippers must be destroyed lest they contaminate his people with their evil teachings. And the Christ said, 'Father, I will do what is necessary to free the peoples of the world, and your name shall become great and everyone will bow down before your might and glory.' And God smiled and was happy."

- extract from the lost 'Book of Pre-emption'

2 October 2002
... A Little Less Conversation

Let me explain a little about Cassandra Barclay and how I met her. Cassandra was born in 1979 when, depending on your point of view, I was either sitting in school learning my eight-times table or coming to the end of a turbulent affair with my own mother. She was the oldest and most attractive of three daughters and destined to break my heart and leave me for dead three and a half years from now.

I knew nothing about Cassandra until I met her during a summer holiday in Clermont-Ferrand in the Auvergne region of France. On that fateful day she ran into me on her bicycle and almost killed the both of us.

I had picked central France for my holiday for the peace and calm, and was still trying to put behind me recent events, especially the deaths of Kieran and that girl in Munich. It was actually the first holiday I'd been on since Thailand and there, as I was walking down a quiet country road, looking around at the black, volcanic mountains and taking in the unspoilt beauty of the countryside, I heard someone shout out behind me and turned, only to be hit by a girl on a bike, coming downhill, out of control and apparently lacking a set of brakes.

I managed to slow her down by selflessly using my body as a crash barrier and together, she, me and the bike fell off the road and rolled down the grassy incline off to one side.

I can remember all too well how mortified the girl was. I'd managed to hit my head on a rock and was dazed by the whole event and all I could hear was her rambling on about how sorry she was and she didn't know how she managed to lose control and oh, God was I all right?

When I didn't answer her I was subjected to a second barrage of questioning, this time in French, and which, unless you're asking me if I speak English, what the time is or to close a door, is all a bit over my head.

Failing to understand a word she was saying I decided it would be best for all concerned if I just got back to bleeding and passed out.

Five or ten minutes later I came back to my senses with her jacket cushioning my head and her very attractive face looking worriedly down at me.

"Am I dead?"

"You're English."

Ah, so the rumours were true. The words 'dead' and 'English' are totally interchangeable. "It certainly sounds that way."

She shook her head at me. "No, I mean that I went through your bags to find ID whilst you were out. Your passport said you were English."

"Ah."

I felt my head, which had a lump on it the size of an ostrich egg, but thankfully the cut didn't seem too deep.

"Sorry, I'm bleeding on your jacket. I'm Julian, by the way." I said, holding out the hand that didn't have blood on it.

"I know," she said, waving my passport at me.

Eventually she calmed down a bit and regained enough of her composure to tell me that her name was Cassandra, though her friends called her Cassie, to which I had asked which name her victims normally used, and she laughed, probably more out of relief that she hadn't killed me than from any love-at-first-sight attraction.

For my part, even with my head pounding, I couldn't deny that I felt more than a slight attraction to this tanned girl in a pair of hot pants and a tight, turquoise t-shirt.

After half an hour of lying there, listening to her, I'd been informed that she was on holiday in France for a month, taking some time out from her job, which was advertising and marketing for her father, who sold some sort of orthopaedic medical equipment in Bromsgrove and made a small fortune from doing so. I told her that I worked for an insurance company and had just managed to get a promotion and was now the guy who told people they weren't going to get any money because their claim was clearly, as the manual politely put it, 'a great steaming pile of bollocks'.

Eventually I felt fit to move and, retrieving her bike, we found that apart from the wheels being bent out of shape and not actually going round, it wasn't too badly bashed up.

She shook her head. "Well, it was only a hire bike. Looks like I'll lose my deposit though."

"But on the plus side, you got to meet me!" I said more chirpily than I felt. Even with the hot sun beating down on me and a concussion setting in, I hadn't missed the fact that she was incredibly good-looking and I wasn't going to risk not seeing her again. And though her outfit didn't leave much to the imagination, I wouldn't mind having the blanks filled in one night after a few drinks back in my hotel room.

We wandered back up the hill, me carrying her bike for her and, since I was in Clermont alone, it was nice to have someone else there from England that I could communicate with. I tried on more than one occasion to show her how good my French was, but she just laughed at my use of phrases such as 'le bike' and 'je m'appelle Jules' and was intrigued, though hardly surprised when I told her that I'd learned all my French from a mixture of subtitled continental movies and endless repeats of *'Allo 'Allo*.

We handed in the bike, much to the consternation of the bloke behind the hire desk, and she explained, though my translation of her French may be a little off, that she'd been hit by an elephant just out of town and it stole all her belongings and please don't be angry as she was just a poor little English girl a long way from home.

And she smiled at him and bunched up her breasts and he dutifully gave her the deposit back and went off to sort out the wheels.

"That was shameless." I said.

"I'm in advertising. I have no moral scruples and know that men will do absolutely anything for breasts."

"You reckon?"

She stood there, folded her arms under her ample chest and calmly asked if I'd like to buy her dinner.

"Sure. Anywhere in particular?"

"How about the most expensive place in town?"

"Anything you say, but I'd just like to point out that my agreeing to this has nothing at all to do with your breasts."

We agreed to meet at eight, back there at the bike hire shop, and I wandered off to my hotel, hoping that my attraction to her wasn't too noticeable through my shorts and thinking that there should be some sort of law that stopped women using their bodies like that.

We met at eight, me wearing a casual shirt, her wearing the most amazing black dress that showed off her cleavage to her best advantage. I had an emergency tie in my pocket in case of a dress code and was studiously not looking at her chest as she took my arm and let me walk her slowly toward the restaurant.

The place we arrived at was called simply *'Bleu'* and, whilst my thoughts since I left her that afternoon had chiefly been about what was under the tight turquoise t-shirt she had been wearing, hers had obviously been along the more sensible lines of ordering a table at one of the most popular places in town.

We were shown to a seat in the window, ideal for watching the evening traffic pass by and close to the door too, in case I needed to make a hasty getaway.

"I hope you appreciate how many strings I had to pull to get us in here at such short notice." She said, picking up the wine list.

"Oh, certainly. Very appreciated. Rest assured." Don't stare at her chest. Don't stare at her chest. Don't. Stare at her chest.

"And I hope you appreciate how much this place charges for dinner." A waiter arrived and she ordered our drinks in fluent French whilst I was mentally adding up how much money was left on my credit card.

"Just so long as I don't need a second mortgage." I didn't tell her that I wasn't even on the property ladder.

"It's not quite that expensive, but I know of a few exclusive bars that will help push up the price later." She scanned the menu. "What are you having?"

I scanned the menu and damn, it was all in French. I knew roughly the French for chicken, ham and beef, and took a stab at one of the dishes that I really hoped was beef in a peppercorn sauce.

The waiter came back, poured a little red wine for me to taste and once it had my much sought-after seal of approval, he topped up our glasses and turned to Cassandra to get the food order. No fool, this one. Clearly knows the difference between an organ grinder and a monkey.

As the phrase 'organ grinder' passed through my mind, I found my eyes wandering back to her cleavage and quickly averted my gaze outside where I intently watched the street for any signs of non-breast related activity.

When the waiter wandered away she told me that she'd ordered us salads to begin with and, though not my first choice for a starter, I thanked her and sat there wondering what to say and trying to get rid of my few remaining first-date nerves.

I took a sip of wine and glanced around at the packed restaurant where couples and the occasional family were dining, discussing life and making their plans for the future. A few tables away from us a French couple were animatedly arguing, him throwing his arms around whilst she slapped her forehead and probably muttered words like *Sacre bleu!* And, just behind them some other French stereotypes were getting up to exactly the sort of thing you'd think they would be doing. All I needed to complete the picture was a guy in a striped top, selling onions and reeking of garlic. And to pull my attention back to the matter at hand I suddenly heard Cassandra say,

"Just to let you know, I never fuck anyone on a first date, no matter how expensive the wine is."

To which I rather wittily replied, "Err, okay."

"You might get a kiss at the end of the night, though I'd expect you to be a gentleman and keep your hands and tongue to yourself."

Rumbled. Now I was looking like a potential rapist.

"I, err, just wanted to buy you dinner. You know, get to know each other better? Make the most of us both being English?" One of these excuses must work. I really didn't want to have to fall back on the time honoured classic, 'I just wanted to get you drunk and see you naked', line. And anyway, strange as it may seem, the more I got to know her, the more I was actually interested in her as a person.

"If it makes you feel less uncomfortable," she continued, "on the second date I'll do pretty much anything."

"Oh." Such a tease! "And the third date?" I was doing my best to stop my voice breaking up.

"We'll see. I just wanted to drive you wild with desire, leave you horny and get you begging for more. Did I mention I was in advertising?"

Thankfully the salads chose that exact moment to turn up as I was starting to feel totally out of my depth.

As I made my way through the various bits of greenery, I was secretly impressed at the way she had me wrapped around her little finger. She knew exactly how to put me in my place, was staying firmly in control and eventually, when she continues the conversation, comes out with the line, "So, you're in insurance? I bet that's a barrel of laughs."

And again, I'm on the defensive and starting to worry that I won't actually make it to the second date, let alone a third.

"Actually, we get some particularly bizarre claims through my department."

"Like pet iguana's escaping from their cages, causing electrical fires and completely destroying the house of someone who's knee deep in debt to the mafia?"

"Something like that, except not so exciting. A bit less Hollywood and a bit more like, 'My washing machine leaked and I need a new carpet.'" And she nodded, happily playing her game, leading me along, taking me exactly where she wants to go and not an inch further.

"So, I'm curious," I say between mouthfuls of leaves and croutons, "Do you use breasts a lot when you advertise orthopaedic medical equipment?"

"These breasts?" she says gathering her cleavage together and pointing at them with her salad fork.

"No, not those exact breasts. Any breasts. I mean, it doesn't strike me as a very sex-led industry."

"You be surprised what it takes to make someone buy a wheel chair!

For example, I can show you two chairs. The first one is blue, a bog-standard, cheap and cheerful number being pushed along by a doctor. It paints a picture in the mind of a potential buyer of honesty, integrity and reliability. "

I pictured a wheelchair being pushed along by Dick Van Dyke from *Diagnosis: Murder*. Don't ask me why.

"The second is a red one. It has the exact same functions of the first one but it's more expensive and carries a higher mark-up. It's modelled by a woman in a kinky nurse's outfit, double-D chest in a half-cup wonder-bra, bright red lipstick and, rather than pushing it along, she's lounging in it, one leg draped over the side, flashing her knickers, with a seductive finger in her mouth. Oh, and she's got a stethoscope just to show that she's a real nurse."

For an even less explainable reason I picture Dick Van Dyke in a nurses outfit, giving me his best 'come hither' smile.

"Which would you buy?"

"Neither. I don't need a wheel chair."

"But if you did, you'd go for the more expensive one sold to you by the boobs."

I shake my head, partly to get rid of the image of a transvestite Dick Van Dyke. "And that's how you sell things for your father?"

"No. that would be stupid, but I did my degree thesis on how to sell flash cars to brainless men and whilst the rules don't apply to everything you want to sell, they do get people to buy you dinner."

"Good point." And the salad is switched for the main course and I find that I'm really, really starting to like this girl.

Over the next week, all that remained of her holiday before she flew home, we met up every day and I took her for dinner a couple more times, though she eventually took pity on my finances and chose less exclusive venues, and on the last day she actually took me out and paid for lunch before giving me her number back home and telling me as she kissed me good-bye that I'd better call her or there'd be serious trouble.

I didn't even mind that she reneged on her second date promise and that by the time we said goodbye at the airport we'd done no more than kiss.

That's how easily I fell in love with Cassandra Louise Barclay.

It was almost a week later when I was packing to start my trip back home that I found out she'd somehow got into my luggage. I didn't notice the missing passport at first, just the note and phone number she'd left in its place.

Now you definitely have to call me.

And smiling, I reached for the phone, sealing my own destiny with every button I pressed.

2002 – 2003

It's voting time again in California as public opinion moves against current Governor, Gray Davis who is recalled from office on the grounds that he was mismanaging pretty much everything he came into contact with.

Davis was accused of overspending, whilst at the same time cutting public funding and endangering safety. Recalling the events leading up to the scandal, one anonymous official remarked that "Davis was totally obsessed with Lee Majors. He used to buy anything and everything he could find on eBay. About a year ago, I was with him when he bid the entire healthcare budget on a signed jumpsuit that Lee wore in the pilot for *The Six Million Dollar Man*."

Pulled from office, Davis was forced to take a back seat as the elections rolled out a batch of celebrity candidates such as actor, Arnold Schwarzenegger, publisher Larry Flynt and little Arnold from *Diff'rent Strokes*.

As the results were counted it became clear that little Arnold was attracting quite a lot of attention with his *'What You Talkin' 'Bout Willis'* comeback tour and when the final numbers came in, the little guy had managed to accumulate over fourteen thousand Republican votes.

Sadly, much as it would have been nice to have pint-sized Gary Coleman running around as Governor, the position went to Arnie the Terminator with a slightly larger majority of 4.2 million ballots in his favour.

Of the one hundred and thirty-five candidates, one hundred and thirty of them shared just three percent of the of the votes and special mention should probably be made of Bob Gibb, Ron Spangler, Bill Thill, Joel Wurth and Jurlene Jeanne Kokoa White, who, despite some quite comical names, only managed to gain just one vote each.

20 March 2003
... One More Chance

I remember that around the time when America was sending troops into Iraq, I had to go away for a couple of days on business to get some sort of insurance claim validated by specialists in London and when I came back home Cassandra, who had moved to Nottingham to help promote her father's second business, was acting more than a little strange.

At the time I accused her having slept with someone else, which she denied, telling me that I was an imbecile and she wasn't going to talk about it any further. I let it slide, realising I was probably over reacting, but after that life never really seemed so stable. The next three years were increasingly marred by arguments, accusations and recriminations until she inevitably packed her bags and cleared out.

In order to save myself from messing up the relationship and having her leave me I came up with a simple plan. On the days I knew that the other me was out of the way, I would take his place and meet up with her, treating her like a princess, apologising for acting like a fool and telling her that everything was all my fault. It would be a bit weird, but I could hopefully smooth over my other self's short-comings and give him and her a chance at working things out.

And the first chance I had was on the day of the Iraq invasion, a day or two before I would have my first major argument with her.

At this time the other me had really short hair and though it had been years since I'd personally sported that look, I went and got myself trimmed and, spying on myself as I left for London, I noted the clothes I was wearing these days and bought some similar ones for myself.

I showered and shaved, picked up a couple of bottles of wine and left the house to go and visit her, though not without a twinge of doubt that maybe I was right all those years ago and perhaps she really was seeing someone else. She might not even be at home, having taken advantage of her free evening to spend it with her mystery lover.

And now I'm standing in front of her door, marvelling at how much it looks just like my memory of it, and I knock, wondering if I can pull this off since in my timeframe I haven't spoken to her for over thirty years and don't have a clue what to say if she asks me things like 'did I enjoy last night's meal?'.

She answers the door, almost exactly as I remember her, wearing a loose t-shirt, this one with the name of some barely known indie-band emblazoned across it. I'm speechless and just stand there looking at her. I'd forgotten quite how beautiful she was and how much of her love for life showed through in her infectious grin. I'd completely forgotten the way that her hair curled around her ears, framing her face and making her sapphire-blue eyes even more intense.

"Julian! What the hell are you doing here? You're supposed to be in London!"

I just smile my best, most charming smile and hold up the bottles.

"Surprise!"

And as I look at her now I realise that yet again I've been lying to myself. I have no real interest in sorting out the relationship between her and the other me. I was just using all that as an excuse to get myself here, to give me a clear-conscience way of getting back into her life. It seems that no matter how good my intentions were when I was sent back in time, I always revert back to type when it comes to getting my own way.

"I cancelled it. Cancelled London. I thought I'd surprise you with a night in and some wine!" She seems a little uncertain, though it's probably just the sudden change in her evening that's being thrust upon her. "Unless you have other things to do?" Like you've invited someone else round whilst I'm working away.

"No! This is great!" And she brushes her hand through her long blonde hair and I'm thinking again, *just don't stare at her chest*, and as she ushers me into the front room there's still a part of me that valiantly and desperately maintains that I'm doing all this for my other self.

She comes back with a couple of glasses and a cork screw and lies on the floor propping herself up on some cushions in front of the gas fire. It's almost April, but the weather's bad and it's still too early to turn off the central heating and I'm sitting on the sofa realising that I look like I'm nervously visiting my grandparents or something, rather than coming round for a nice romantic evening in.

I open the wine and pour out two glasses, again amazed at my own gullibility. Amazed that I'd managed to fool myself into thinking that a nice quiet romantic night in with my girl friend wasn't going to wind up in the bedroom and that I was doing all of this to promote better relations between her and the other Julian, who is no doubt in London right now, pissed off and bored in his hotel room. And I know that's exactly what he's doing, because I was there myself thirty-six years ago. Pissed off, bored and watching hotel TV whilst wondering where to go for dinner all by myself.

And I hand Cassie a glass and she picks up the remote to turn off *EastEnders* and pats her lap, indicating that perhaps I should come over and cuddle up a bit.

As I settle down with her she strokes my stomach and says, "You're putting on weight!"

"Still as full of compliments as ever, I see! I think it's the stress of being with you, forcing me to comfort eat."

I rest against her, as low as I can whilst still being able to drink, painfully aware of how close my head is to her chest. I can smell her perfume, a fragrance I haven't encountered in over three decades but which instantly brings back every memory of her I thought I'd forgotten.

"So what was so important that you had to cancel your trip and come over here?"

There was no point in lying when the truth would work perfectly well.

"I was missing you. I didn't want to leave you alone today, so I'll go tomorrow, work twice as fast and still be back for the weekend."

And she just leans over and kisses me full on the lips and I remember just exactly how much I've been missing and it's horribly obvious to me right now that there hasn't been a woman in my life since Diane left me. I return the kiss, years of repressed passion finding their way to the surface, overwhelming her through this single intimate contact.

It seems like forever until she breaks away.

"You *are* missing me!" And she takes a sip from her wine and playfully squeezes me through my jeans.

Sorry, Julian, but I think it's finally dawning on me why your relationship got a bit rocky. First I cheat on my dad, now I'm cheating on myself. And right now, with the prospect, the certainty, of sleeping with Cassie on the cards, I really don't care.

And what do I do about saving Julian's relationship? How do I stop him from annoying Cassie to the point where in three years' time she'll leave him? I suppose I can work on that in the morning.

I'm about to reach up and stroke her face when the silence is shattered by the harsh tones of the phone ringing in the hallway. I almost knock her drink out of her hand as I jump up, like a guilty schoolboy caught doing something he shouldn't be doing in the girls changing rooms. My thoughts flash back to that night down in London and I know for certain that it's me calling.

"Don't answer it!" I say, a little too loud and quick.

"Why? It might be important. I'm expecting my dad to call with some details of a new deal he wants me to work on." And she heads to the hallway and I can see everything going terribly wrong and I'm wondering which part of me thought that this was in any way a good idea.

The horny part. The part that hasn't had sex in almost four years.

I strain to hear what she's saying, trying to gauge what the reaction will be when my other self hears that he's supposedly in two places.

And then she's back here with me saying, "Wrong number," and my paranoia takes a back seat, though I make a mental note to accidentally disconnect the phone when I go upstairs to use the toilet.

There's no time like the present and I excuse myself, head upstairs, go through the motions, wash my hands, back downstairs, yank out the phone cord, (which I have to remember to plug in again when I leave tomorrow morning), and back into the front room where Cassie is stretched out on the rug wearing just her underwear, her t-shirt and jeans tossed casually on the sofa.

"It was getting warm." She smiles at me and no amount of *don't-look-at-her-chest*-ing is going to stop me this time. "Care to join me?" She holds out her arms and I snuggle in close and we kiss and slowly my shirt is unbuttoned and my belt tugged undone and my trousers are unzipped as my tongue probes her mouth.

And I'm thinking, I'm sorry Julian, really sorry Julian, over and over for about a minute until she breaks off the kiss and moves down to take me in her mouth, at which point the part of my brain that so cunningly orchestrated this evening tells the stupid, honourable part of me to shut up and enjoy the ride.

Any anyway, she's still technically my girlfriend.

Twenty minutes later and I'm sweating, panting and lying beside her, wondering if it would break the mood if I got up to turn off the fire. My heart's beating away far too fast in my chest and it's been so long since I was expected to perform with anyone that I'm beginning to fear some sort of seizure.

"You look like you haven't been fucked in ages!" she says. "You're getting out of shape."

"I'll try harder next time! Want to go upstairs?"

And she does and we hit the bed, and this time it's slower, and I spend what seems like hours paying attention to every inch of her body and by the time we finally fall asleep it's almost three in the morning and I'm thinking that my younger self has got a bit more to live up to now, and also that I have to remember to plug the phone back in on my way out tomorrow morning.

2003 - 2004

And so Saddam is finally captured, hiding out in a hole, desperately trying to hide his stash of classic seventies pornography from the advancing US troops whilst, back in America, President Bush is still trying to find the best way of telling everyone that there was no actual proof at all that Iraq held Weapons of Mass Destruction.

As events turn out, US intelligence had been given a tip-off that Saddam was in possession of *'Barely Legal Big Ones'* and *'Weapons of Mass Eruption'*, both of which were mistakenly assumed to be code words for nuclear or biological weapons programmes but turned out to be the artistically justified exploits of Big Jim Wang and his sidekicks Clitty Galore and Candy Cumshots.

On his arrest, Saddam claimed that he was 'just looking after them for a friend.'

Elsewhere in the world, things aren't improving much as a twelve year old Japanese girl is murdered by her eleven year old classmate. Apparently the younger girl was upset by something posted about her on the internet so she fell out with her friend and slit her throat with a knife.

And as if that wasn't insane enough, the killer has been turned into an internet icon and actually has websites devoted to manga-style 'fan' art and has message boards discussing her actions and venerating her as some sort of cult hero.

The murderer, dubbed 'Nevada-tan' by her followers did, however, issue an apology for her actions and remarked that if she'd though it through properly she wouldn't have done it.

Oh. Well I suppose that makes it all okay then.

5 June 2004
... I Know I Won't Be Leaving Here

I've ended up spending more than a year impersonating myself and building up what I thought was a better relationship with Cassie, smoothing over arguments that she's had with the other me, whilst at the same time causing several more arguments between them when he couldn't remember certain things they'd done together.

I've kept it down to maybe once or twice a month, I didn't want to push it too far, or give either of them too many things to figure out. I didn't particularly want the other Julian thinking he was going crazy. But I just couldn't stay away from Cassie. It was like shoplifting. You manage to get away with it once so you go and do it again, and then once more, and then yet again, until you eventually get caught.

I came close on a few occasions, but no matter how unlikely it seemed that either Cassie or Julian would be able to explain why he was in two places at the same time, they always did. Or perhaps they just ignored it. As I said, my interference only occasionally sparked off a major argument.

So a year has passed and things are fast coming to a head and I know that it won't be long now before the relationship gets stressed and Cassie will leave Julian and I'm no longer sure how much I'm to blame for that happening, either as the original me, or the older, not much wiser version.

I feel like my hands are tied. Cassie has intoxicated me with her beauty, her charm and her intelligence. Unlike Jenny, she knows where she's going in life and knows exactly how to get what she wants. Unlike Diane she doesn't live in the shadow of a past she can never fully come to terms with. And as a bonus, she's got an incredible body and a bigger sexual appetite than both of them put together.

Which is why, after a long year of deliberation, I've come to the conclusion that I need to be with her more than my other self does.

I've been back into my own past and watched me grow from a baby into a messed up adult. I knew firsthand what it was like to never really know my mother and later found out what it was like to know her completely and then lose her again. I've seen the mistakes I made get replayed over and over and know that the Julian I was back in 2006 is nothing like the man I am today. I have seventy years of experience in this body and whilst the younger me is beginning to destroy his relationship with Cassie, I know that only I have the power to mend it and set it back on track. I can be a better lover and perhaps even a better husband to Cassie than the other me ever could.

In thirty-four years of thinking that I've come back to save myself it suddenly comes as something of a shock when I realise that I'm actually here to replace him. All I need to do is remove him from the picture, take his place and Cassie will never leave and we all get to live happily ever after.

Everyone except my other self, of course, but that's okay because in a way, he'll still be a part of me.

Having figured all that out there really isn't much left for me to do. I just have to find a way to get rid of my competition. And the sooner the better since, with every passing day, my useless counterpart gets ever closer to screwing up my last best chance at happiness. If I don't act soon everything I've learned from being with Jenny, whatever my time with Diane has taught me, all the things I've gained from my second chance at life will all go to waste If I don't replace Julian in Cassie's life.

It will all be so simple.

I call myself on the phone and listen as that stupid voice of his answers. The guy doesn't even sound like me. He has no right ruining the future I could have with Cassie.

"Julian, I need to see you. I have some information regarding your mother. Meet me tonight at Phoenix Park. Catch the last tram. I'll be waiting for you by the big stone."

I give him no time to answer or raise any questions. It's simply an order and I know how much he misses his mother. He won't pass up the opportunity to meet me and, although I don't remember making any journeys to Phoenix Park that year, I know in my heart that this time the future really can be changed. This is why I'm here.

It's after midnight and the last tram has just pulled in and Julian is on the platform, looking around for whomever it is he's supposed to meet. I look up at the angel for advice, but she's just silently watching me, still blurred and indistinct, still silver-blue and cold as ice.

I have his mobile number and call him, watching as he reaches into his jacket pocket and flicks open his phone.

"Yes?"

"Wait until the tram has gone back out and then head up toward the stone on the traffic island." And again I hang up on him, hoping the conversation is short enough for him to not recognise his own voice.

And the angel, my constant companion over the past few years fades away, leaving me to speak to him alone and do what has to be done.

He walks up the path and I wait until he's close enough for me to hear his breathing before stepping out of the shadows and confronting him. He almost trips and falls when he sees me, almost the mirror image of himself. He's presented with a man looking just like him, the same style of clothes, similar boots, black jeans and a shirt. Even the hair style is the same. Even our shirts are similar shades of red.

"Hello, Julian." I say, wondering what he will think, whether his mind will put things together and work out that I've been following him since he was born. I can't help but feel a little sad. We share the same name and the same life, but unfortunately there's now only room for one of us.

He's incredulous, speechless. How do you address someone who looks almost exactly like you? A twin perhaps, separated at birth? The easiest explanation, even if an unlikely one.

"Who the hell are you?"

I walk over and place a hand on his shoulder, half expecting a jolt of electricity to pass between us. It's just like taking hold of a long lost brother.

"Do you have to ask? After all this time? I watched you grow up, looked after you so many times when you were young."

Recognition falls into place, somehow he ignores my similarity to himself and leaps at the alternatives. "Julian Grey? You met me that time in town, at the pub. You had a beard. You knew my parents?"

"I was a good friend of your father and I loved your mother with all my heart. I used to read bedtime stories to you and treated you like a little brother. But you know there's more to it than that. How old do you think I am? I can't be all that much older than you. Look at me. You know that something isn't 'normal' here."

He's looking at me in disbelief and since I know the way he thinks, I know he's thinking of something Sherlock Holmes once said; 'once you've eliminated the impossible, whatever is left, no matter how improbable, must be the truth.'

"Am I impossible, Julian?" I ask.

"You," he's stumbling but there really is no other possible explanation. "You're me."

"You want to know how?" I put an arm around his shoulders, "Let's walk."

And we move up the path a little further toward some trees, a good way from the lights and the few passing cars.

And I try to explain to him that he's messing up his life, that if he doesn't change now he'll carry on messing it up and he'll die lonely and tired and unfulfilled.

I tell him that in a year or so he will finally annoy Cassie so much that she leaves him and he'll think that it's all over, that his life has been for nothing and on that night, on this very spot, he will be given another chance, a chance to go back and make things right.

"And that's why you're here?" He asks me, still trying to make sense of a ridiculous situation. "To make things right? To show me what I need to do to make Cassie stay?"

Even now I can see that he's far too naive, that he really doesn't have what it takes to make this life work out. I was hoping there'd be some other way, but it's clear that this version of me is way too stupid to sort things out with Cassie.

"No. You see, I've been there already, I've been back to when you, when I, was born and had the chance to make a difference and all I did was look out for my own interests and make everything more complicated. You were right when you accused me of messing up your parent's marriage. I've gone on and messed up my own marriage and even my presence here is messing up your future. And it's only now that I've finally managed to figure out the truth.

"You just aren't old enough or clever enough to make the right decisions on your own."

He's shocked and doesn't know what to say. "But you can guide me! You can show me what to do!"

"No, Julian! I've been there, remember! I've been you aged forty, aged fifty, aged sixty and you will never learn! You just continually fuck up everything you get involved with and it's only now that things can finally be put straight. You're going to have to go away, Julian."

And he's worried and starting to panic as I grab hold of him and hug him, giving him one last thing to hold on to in the world, one last chance to show him that everything will work out okay.

He nervously returns the hug and, as I hold on to him, one arm around his shoulders, he barely even feels the sting of steel as I drive a knife through his back and into his heart.

He stiffens and releases his grip and I lower him down to the floor. And the angel appears again from nowhere.

"What now?" I ask.

"Go back home." She says. "It isn't quite over yet."

And she and my other self's body vanish into thin air, leaving me with a long walk back home.

2004 – 2005

No matter how outrageous some claim the invasion of Iraq to have been, when the public are given a chance to vote for a new President more than half of the American voters gave their support once again to George Bush, securing him a second term in office. Now George has four more years to do whatever he pleases with the world, and this time he no longer has to worry about getting re-elected.

No, this time around George just has to make excuses for why a city like New Orleans, which is mostly below sea-level and prone to hurricanes, hasn't got a reasonable defence against flooding. I suppose when you're a man like George it's difficult to envisage floods like those ever actually occurring.

In London, terrorists attack the capital and explode suicide bombs on the public transport system, prompting the police to over-react and gun down anything that looks vaguely foreign.

Back in the States, pop star Michael Jackson is acquitted of child molestation charges and, whilst he in all probability didn't really do anything, the public are still left wondering how anyone with a history like his can really be stupid enough to let unsupervised children sleep with him in his bed.

23 November 2005
... I'm Not Broke, But You Can See the Cracks

I managed to persuade Cassie to move in with me, to share my house in the countryside, and finally everything was falling into place and was right with my world. I gave her everything she needed and she, in return, completed me. Without the other Julian around to mess things up I was free to enjoy the most rewarding relationship I'd ever had in my life.

Even my guardian angel had disappeared.

There was just one incident that unsettled me, a month or so ago, when Cassie had to go back down south for a week to help her father on a new campaign. For some reason she wanted to go alone and I didn't want to be apart and we argued and she told me that I was smothering her and she needed some space away from me.

She flared up at me, told me to 'stop being so fucking possessive.'

So I let her go alone and things were pretty normal when she got back, but I can't help wondering if there's still something I'm missing.

I keep asking her if everything is okay, and she tells me there's no problem. But she gets more irritable than she used to and she's started to smoke, which she knows I hate.

I keep telling her that I'm there if she needs me, and I am, but she never asks me for any help. I have to at least consider the possibility that she's getting all the help she needs from someone else.

Then again, on other days, I'm fairly certain I'm just over-reacting. I mean, now I've got rid of my other self things should be more than settled. What do I have to worry about?

So why do I feel like I'm trying to convince myself of something?

And how come I've started to wake up occasionally thinking I can hear something scratching in the bedroom?

There's less than six months now until the day Cassie left and I went to Phoenix Park and got pissed out of my face. I suppose I'm just worried that it could all happen again.

Last night I dreamed that I was in bed with Cassie, except every time I looked again it wasn't her, it was Diane or Jenny. And the angel was watching me from the corner of the room, her wings outstretched behind her and her voice echoing around inside my head, saying words that I couldn't quite make out.

And Jenny or Diane or Cassie was kissing me and whispering in my ear.

"It's over."

And I find myself praying that, six months from now, it finally is.

Endings

"...imagine a puddle waking up one morning and thinking, 'This is an interesting world I find myself in - an interesting hole *I find myself in - fits me rather neatly, doesn't it? In fact it fits me staggeringly well, must have been made to have me in it!' This is such a powerful idea that as the sun rises in the sky and the air heats up and as, gradually, the puddle gets smaller and smaller, it's still frantically hanging on to the notion that everything's going to be alright, because this world was* meant *to have him in it, was* built *to have him in it; so the moment he disappears catches him rather by surprise. I think this may be something we need to be on the watch-out for."*

- Douglas Adams, as quoted in his eulogy
delivered by Richard Dawkins in 2001

19 November 2006
... Fade to Grey

There's nothing in the house left to smash.

I find once again that the world never really changes and it seems that I change least of all. After all my posturing, after my claims that I could be the one to save my own future, after actually going so far as to murder myself, everything simply returns to type.

Things were going so well for Cassie and me. We were a wonderful team. I doted on her, gave her everything she wanted and for a time there it looked like we could actually make it. This close to the date I was sent back in time, everything still seemed salvageable.

And then this morning she tells me she's leaving. She tells me she doesn't love me anymore and she tells me there's no one else in her life right now, it's just that she doesn't want to be with me. I made it all too easy, I was too much of a walkover. I gave her so much freedom that she lost first her respect for me, and then her love.

It's all happening to me again and enduring it again feels a hundred times worse than the first time she walked out on me.

Cassie meant the world to me and now she's gone again. This is the end result of two lifetimes of causing hurt and pain for so many people. Seventy-two years of mistakes just to find my way back here so I could screw everything up a second time.

My mother is gone. And at the back of my mind I suppose I always knew that she was dead. I ignored the clues all the time, choosing to believe that there was always a chance she'd come back in to my life and make up for not being around when I needed her.

My father's life is a wreck, a shadow of what it could have been had I not been around. He's just another victim of my selfish ego, of my self-centred, nothing's-important-but-me view of life.

My sister's a bit of a mess, but she hasn't had much to do with me so perhaps she'll survive intact. She's got a husband and the kids to keep her going, so maybe Marie will still manage to turn out okay.

And even a facet of my own life, the original 'me', blessed with so much opportunity and vitality has been wiped out. Overwritten.

Now there's only me. A wasted second chance with a future I can't change and the knowledge that whatever I do, I always end up hurting someone I love.

I've had enough and it really is time to finally give in. Whatever destiny has in store it can just go ahead and throw it at me. I'll either survive or I won't. I'll make it one way or another. I have enough money left in my bank account to go away, to begin afresh somewhere else.

I wrap a shirt around the elements of a cheap electric heater I've bought and set a timer to switch it on in fifteen minutes time. And as I leave the house for the last time, the smell of petrol almost overpowers me, but I close the door and lock it with a distant smile playing over my lips.

I catch a bus into town, never bothering to look back.

By the time the house burns down, I'll be very, very drunk and a long way from here.

20 November 2006
... Epilogue

It all begins and ends at Phoenix Park.
Still not a real park, of course, just a business park. Still the terminus of the tramline from the city and still, as the conductor assured me as he roused me from a drunken sleep, 'The end of the line'.

So I'm sitting on the grassy bank, staring at the huge horizontal stone altar and again, it's been a long night. Too many bars, too many beers and, after a short stop-off to re-stock, two fresh bottles of scotch to wash down a box of a hundred prescription painkillers that Cassie had left behind. It will be interesting to see how many I can get through before I pass out.

I have the strangest sense of *déjà vu* and it's cold and dark, and I'm drunk and I'll probably catch my death from the cold. And for what seems like the second time in my life, it's all down to Cassandra Louise Barclay.

Again it's just me and a couple of pretty much empty bottles of scotch slouching here, and I'm up to twenty tablets and I'm staring at this increasingly malevolent rock, wondering if it too feels like it's been through all this before.

At least, I think as I throw another ten pills down my throat for good measure, I'll always have my self-pity.

"It could all have been different."

Ah. The arrival of my constant, silver-blue companion. My guardian angel. "Fat lot of good you turned out to be."

"You've been talking to yourself for the past two hours. I couldn't help but overhear."

"You should have spoken up sooner, you could have had a drink."

My mind catches itself as I know I've said these lines before. I look at the two bottles and the numerous empty plastic pill strips lying on the grass by my feet. "There're a couple of mouthfuls left if you want some."

She steps out from her hiding place into the moonlight and, sometime in the early hours of a cold November night, this blurry, naked angel, silver in the glow from the moon stands over me once more.

"I'm here to help you." She says.

And the *déjà vu* feeling gets a hundred times worse. "You," I say as if I'm reading lines from a script, "are one very indistinct, but very naked, woman. If you're about to make me an offer then I'm unlikely to refuse, but you should know that I spent my last cash on the bottles there, and I might not be in much of a state to perform."

And I'm so drunk that I suddenly find myself lying face-down on the grass and she's crouching next to me, a discarded red and yellow pain-killer capsule resting beside her perfectly formed toes.

"Julian, I want you to listen to me very carefully." And she pauses before leaning in close and whispering, "It's all over."

I'm so drunk that I really don't have a clue what's going on. So very drunk. "I just want to go home." I almost sob.

"You've made mistakes, Julian, lots of mistakes. It's time to put them right."

I try to look at her again, but it's all just swimming and blurring and I'm fighting against the nausea in my stomach that's reminding me that everything is finally rushing to a close.

And there's blood on the grass as I'm throwing up and I'm murmuring things to myself and I'll do whatever it takes if you'll just make it stop.

I feel worse than I've ever felt before in my life, yet strangely at peace.

And as the angel fades and darkness finally crashes in on me, the only thought left running through my head is that it all ends at Phoenix Park.

Song Credits
... Seventies

Let It Be - The Beatles - 1970
Riders on the Storm - The Doors - 1971
American Pie - Don McLean - 1972
Stuck in the Middle with You - Steelers Wheel - 1973
Waterloo - ABBA - 1974
Jive Talkin' - The Bee Gees - 1975
Don't Fear the Reaper - Blue Oyster Cult - 1976
God Save The Queen - The Sex Pistols - 1977
Psycho Killer - Talking Heads - 1978
Heart of Glass - Blondie - 1979

Song Credits
... Eighties

Ashes to Ashes - David Bowie - 1980
Start Me Up - The Rolling Stones - 1981
Centerfold - J Geils Band - 1982
This Charming Man - The Smiths - 1983
Two Tribes - Frankie Goes To Hollywood - 1984
Money for Nothing - Dire Straits - 1985
Rock Me, Amadeus - Falco - 1986
Luka - Suzanne Vega - 1987
Dignity - Deacon Blue - 1988
Orange Crush - REM - 1989

Song Credits
... Nineties

U Can't Touch This - MC Hammer - 1990
Smells Like Teen Spirit - Nirvana - 1991
Under the Bridge - Red Hot Chili Peppers - 1992
What's Up? - 4 Non Blondes - 1993
Basket Case - Green Day - 1994
Lump - The Presidents of the United States - 1995
Don't Look Back in Anger - Oasis - 1996
Bittersweet Symphony - The Verve - 1997
Lost in Space - Apollo 440 - 1998
Pretty Fly (For a White Guy) - The Offspring - 1999

Song Credits
... Millennium

All the Small Things - Blink 182 - 2000
19-2000 (Soulchild Remix) - Gorillaz - 2001
A Little Less Conversation - Elvis Presley vs JXL - 2002
Laura - Scissor Sisters - 2003
Take Me Out - Franz Ferdinand - 2004
All Because of You - U2 - 2005
Bad Day - Daniel Powter - 2006

...About the Book

Phoenix Park started out in November 2005 as a desperate attempt to finally start, *and actually finish*, a novel and get myself into print. After a month of writing it was painfully apparent that I was going to need more time to polish things up so I decided to give up my nice, safe office job and live off my fairly meagre savings.

Six months later I reviewed my position. On the plus side I was now the proud owner of a reasonably finished manuscript. On the down side, I'd spent more than my savings and was about to get kicked out on the street by my then-girlfriend for being such a time-wasting layabout.

Still, all things considered, I had my manuscript and a new, exciting life ahead of me so things weren't really all that bad.

Of course, none of the agents I sent my sample chapters to were in the least bit interested in getting my book printed, indeed, most of them didn't even bother to get me a rejection letter printed. And then, whilst spring cleaning my computer one day, I managed to accidentally delete the file containing my final draft and somehow I'd never found the time to make a backup.

The fate of my great novel seemed sealed. All I had left were two lever-arch files containing my double-line spaced final manuscript. I suppose I could have typed it all in again, but the urge to change things would be too great. The novel ended up on a shelf to gather dust.

Then this year, after a furious month of scanning in the pages, converting them to Word documents and painstakingly editing the resulting files, the novel was once again ready to move forward. Sadly, I don't have the benefit of an editor, a proof reader, or a legal department, but I've done my best and though I'm certain a few typos have slipped through the net, I'm pretty happy with the result.

Now I just have to find a printer...

Gabriel Wood
30 November 2008

...About the Author

Much like his fictional creation, Gabriel Wood has spent much of his life in Leicestershire and Nottinghamshire and has spent most of his adult years desperately trying to convince people that he's some sort of writer whilst showing all the outward signs of being a reasonably competent Certified Accountant.

Now living happily with his wife and daughter he dreams of that difficult second novel, always assuming of course that he eventually found a printer for his first one.

Mr Wood wishes to point out that although some events taking place in *Phoenix Park* are very roughly based on things that happened to him, his novel remains a work of fiction.

He also wishes to make it perfectly clear, that despite a lot of totally unfounded gossip, he has never been romantically involved with his own mother.

www.ingramcontent.com/pod-product-compliance
Lightning Source LLC
Chambersburg PA
CBHW051750040426
42446CB00007B/304